This is a timely book th[at speaks] today with the question [of which] children to go when others get to stay? As one who has [been on both] sides of this leaving/staying routine, I know the paradoxical feelings that accompany the family separations that are part of missions—including the anger! As a teen, I was the Stayer. As an adult, I was the Goer. As a mom of adult children, I was again the Stayer, saying goodbye to our daughter and son-in-law who would soon be having our first grandchild an ocean away. At that point, I asked God, "Has our family not yet given enough?" But I also know the blessings that spring from this life and how God does indeed keep his promise to return a hundredfold what we have given to him through this obedience, both in this life and in the life to come. Read this book and be blessed in your own journey of watching your children fulfill their calling despite the separations it has cost you.

— **Ruth E. Van Reken**,
co-author of *Third Culture Kids: Growing Up Among Worlds*, author of *Letters Never Sent*, co-founder of Families in Global Transition

Few of us expect our children to move halfway around the world. So when God calls them to do just that in service to him, it can be a difficult and disorienting journey. Not only has Tori Haverkamp traveled this road, but she's also taken field notes to share with you. Writing with humor, wisdom, honesty, and grace, Tori is a skilled guide for the "missionary mama" terrain. These pages are filled with tested advice for the missionary mama's spiritual, relational, emotional, and practical needs.

— **Eric Schumacher**,
author of *Ours: Biblical Comfort for Men Grieving Miscarriage* and *Worthy: Celebrating the Value of Women* (with Elyse Fitzpatrick)

What I see in this book, again and again, is how God is using Tori's pain and heartache for his glory. She doesn't just reach out to other

Missionary Mamas so they can commiserate together; she also points them to Jesus in the middle of their trials. And that's really what we all need. Always.

— **Andrea Warren**,
Language and Culture Director for Campus2Campus

This book is a labor of love and a wealth of wisdom. For any parents working through how to love and support their missionary kids, the perspective Tori shares will help you tremendously. Tori has been a constant source of encouragement to me as a pastor. I pray as you read this book that you will experience a similar burst of encouragement and grace.

— **Mark Vance**,
Lead Pastor at Cornerstone Church of Ames

After reading just a few pages of this book, I thought to myself, "Where was this book six years ago?!" THIS is the book I needed to read as I sobbed at night, alone with my thoughts and aching heart. The tears came from feeling pride in my child's position, from missing them, and from simply being absent for so many of their life milestones. This book is full of personal content, but the literal journey it takes the reader on is so very informative and comforting. It resonated deeply with me. I am sure it will resonate with many others!

— **Diane Hamer**,
Missionary Mama and CAPM at RR Donnelley Company

I am not a Missionary Mama, but if I ever become one, I will keep a copy of this book on my nightstand, and it will likely be dog-eared, underlined, and highlighted. As an experienced backpacker (though not nearly as experienced as Tori), I loved the metaphors that came out of her wilderness adventures. She does an excellent job of combining storytelling with practical information, making this both an entertaining and educational read and an important resource for parents who are releasing their grown kids out into the world of missions.

— **Kim Harms**,
author of *Life Reconstructed: Navigating the World of Mastectomies and Breast Reconstruction*

This book is a practical, easy-to-read guide that all Missionary Mamas can relate to and learn from. I wish this book had been around to help me understand what the stayer goes through when I first went abroad. The journey on which Tori leads us helps us all see how we can bring glory to God as his children, whether we are a goer or stayer.

— **Alishia**,
career missionary and Missionary Mama

Transitions and changes are often difficult, especially when they involve your children. When your child chooses to follow Jesus to a distant country, the change can be even more emotionally challenging. This book gives parents needed encouragement and guidance as they travel this path. Not only does *Missionary Mama's Survival Guide* provide useful tools to help parents grow emotionally and spiritually, but it also offers creative ways to stay connected and involved with your children. (Bonus reward: you will learn more about hiking than you thought you would ever need to know!)

— **Troy Nesbitt**,
Director of The Salt Network

Tori is the real deal. She is a follower of Jesus and a speaker of the truths of the Bible. Whether she is sitting with a friend, mentoring a young woman, facilitating a class, or teaching in a foreign country, Tori authentically shares her life with wisdom and practical application of God's Word. In *Missionary Mama's Survival Guide*, Tori relates the joys and challenges of being a goer's mama. It is an honest, helpful, and delightful book— a great resource for those navigating the Missionary Mama journey.

— **Sarah Stevenson**,
counselor and chaplain at Abide Biblical Counseling for Women

Tori Haverkamp understands the heartache of sending a child into missions. An advocate and comrade, Tori longs to help other parents accept what might feel like an unexpected path for their child and discover the true joy of God's glorious call for their family. May this book bring you comfort.

— **Laura Wifler**,
author, podcaster, and co-founder of Risen Motherhood

The Missionary Mama's Survival Guide

The Missionary Mama's Survival Guide

*Compassionate Help for the
Mothers of Cross-Cultural Workers*

TORI R. HAVERKAMP

© 2023 BY TORI R. HAVERKAMP

All rights reserved. Except for brief quotations in critical publications or review, no part of this book may be reproduced in any manner without prior written permission from the publisher. Write to:

Permissions, The Upstream Collective
P.O. Box 23871
Knoxville, TN 37933

www.theupstreamcollective.org

ISBN: 978-1-7343705-7-7

Printed in the United States of America

All Scripture quotations, unless otherwise indicated, are taken from the Holy Bible, New International Version®, NIV ® Copyright © 1973, 1978, 1984, 2011 by Biblica, Inc.® Used by permission.

Editor: David McWhite
Cover and Interior design:
Hayley Moss, Moss Photo and Design, LLC
hayleyrmoss@gmail.com

I dedicate this book,
the firstfruits of my labor,
to God, the ultimate Missionary Parent.

"All my springs are in you."
(Psalm 87:7 ESV)

— TRH

CONTENTS

Foreword	13
Introduction	17

PART 1: WHERE AM I GOING?

1: An Unfamiliar Journey	25
2: Charting the Path	29

PART 2: HOW WILL I GET THERE?

3: Learning the Lingo	39
4: Training for the Trail	51
5: Following the Cairns	61

PART 3: WHY IS THIS SO HARD?

6: Hot Spots and Blisters	71
7: False Summits, Suffering, and True Views	79
8: "Grandma" Is My Trail Name	85

PART 4: WHAT DO I DO NOW?

9: Living Outside	95
10: A Woman in the Wild	101
11: Trail Magic for You	107
12: Trail Magic for Them	115

PART 5: WHEN WILL THE JOURNEY END?

13: Beyond GPS	121
14: Sharing the Campsite	129
15: Sky Hiking	137

Conclusion	151
Acknowledgments	157
About the Author	159

APPENDIX

FAQs	163
Helpful Resources: Ranger Station	169
Scriptures to Show You the Way	177
References	183
Endnotes	187

FOREWORD

I couldn't move another inch. The climb to the summit of Grays Peak was steady and strenuous. My leg muscles felt the 3,600 feet gain in elevation. At 14,270 feet my two hiking partners and I took in the view as we ate our peanut butter and honey sandwiches.

We had crossed a small creek, navigated a boulder field, trekked through uneven talus, and maneuvered a series of steep and rocky switchbacks. There were moments when standing had not been an option. As we ate and rested, our eyes were drawn to our next challenge: Grays' twin, Torreys. The two mountains are connected by a narrow piece of land called a saddle, which acts as a bridge between the two peaks.

My eyes snapped shut. Saddles have drop-offs on both sides. This is not a welcome sight for a person who has a fear of heights. One of my hiking partners had thoroughly researched the hike. She prepared me for the saddle, and I came up with a strategy to negotiate this. I planned to keep my eyes on the pair of feet in front of me rather than observe the danger on either side of me.

Grays and Torreys are the ninth and eleventh highest mountains in Colorado, respectively. The saddle between them is a little less than a mile long, and many hikers tackle the twins on the same day. Both mountains are considered a class two on a scale where five is the most difficult. That said, there is nothing easy about hiking up a mountain, let alone two.

I wondered, "Can I do a final push and summit Torreys too?" I didn't feel like it. I was tired and achy. My companions, on the other hand, were eager to go. Reluctantly, I forced my leg muscles to stand, and I followed. Thankfully, God gave me a second wind.

We needed to hike down Grays a bit before ascending Torreys. Our descent brought us to a narrower and less stable trail. We navigated more rocks and did a little scrambling. We paid close attention to our footing on the additional 4.55 miles that led us to Torreys Peak at 14,267 feet.

By God's grace, I did it. I made it. I summited two mountains in one day! I totally earned the view. I was thankful I had my hiking poles and friends. Good equipment, solid information, plus the right hiking partners made the two-fers doable.

Life as a mom is like summiting two mountains. We expect the first. We prepare for those initial eighteen years. But we are reluctant to summit a second mountain, the one where our kids are adults, adults who might choose a path we did not expect. We were ready to descend and enjoy these years. We were not prepared to experience another challenge, a challenge that involves physical separation. It feels a bit unfair.

When my daughter and son-in-love were first married, they went on a mission trip where they traveled the contiguous United States in an RV named Mavis. Their Do Good Project took them across the country to meet and interview people who own nonprofits. During that year they missed birthdays, Christmas, Easter, and other family gatherings. Our phone conversations were limited.

The lack of connection to and reduced contact with our kids grieves our mama's heart. If you picked up this book, then you most likely have an adult child who has chosen the mission path, a path that will last longer than my daughter's. Your child will miss family celebrations, and communication will be limited. It's likely grandchildren will enter the equation, and you will have to navigate living away from them as well. This is not the family portrait you expected.

Their choice, not yours, forces the second summit. This is the mountain you are reluctant to climb. You did not prepare for twin summits. This journey was not part of your plans for your child.

You find you have to adjust your expectations, push your fears aside, increase your faith, and refocus. As you make your way on a path you would not have chosen, you need the right equipment, lingo, research, and a faith-filled guide to come alongside you.

Tori is that compassionate and knowledgeable guide for moms who have a Goer. She does not offer platitudes; instead, she provides real-life experience and applicable, practical ways to navigate this difficult journey. She intimately knows this path and its pitfalls. She understands the mixture of emotion that comes when a child is a cross-cultural worker.

This book will give you a new perspective on your child's call and your role as a Missionary Mama. Tori will help you open your hands to God's will and prepare your heart for his way. She will encourage you to trust God. He is the one who can give you the second wind you need to summit the second mountain.

Missionary Mama, you've got this because God is with you and with your child. Just keep your eyes fixed on Tori's feet. She will show you how to avoid drop-offs so you may travel well on this unexpected journey.

May God bless you and your Goer.

— Lori Wildenberg

Lori is the author of six parenting books, including "Messy Journey: How Grace and Truth Offer the Prodigal a Way Home" and "Messy Hope: Help Your Child Overcome Anxiety, Depression, or Suicidal Ideation". You can find more information on Lori, her resources, and parent coaching at her website, loriwildenberg.com.

INTRODUCTION

During the spring of 2020, I took a Missiology class to finish my Master of Theological Studies degree. As a final project, we were to design a workable mission program for our local church. Since our church already had a good model for national and international missions, I decided to change the rules, which is what I always do with assignments—or recipes or sewing patterns—often with limited success. This time, however, I changed the rules of the assignment because I thought I had a better idea (which is also always the case).

Being twenty-five years older than the average seminary student and also the mother of a missionary gave me a unique perspective on missions that my missiology cohorts didn't have. I wanted to design a mission program not for the "Goers" (this is a term I will use often in the book to designate the missionary) but for the *parents* of the Goers—the "Stayers." Specifically, I had a heart for the mothers of missionaries. Here is an excerpt from my project:

> As a missionary mom, I have few other parents who can relate to my situation. And although I am in awe

of the great God who chose my child to go on mission abroad, I often let the sadness of his absence eclipse the wonder of his position. With the addition of a daughter-in-law and now a granddaughter, the longing for closeness—for sharing life together—has become even more pronounced. I think this longing for family togetherness is God-ordained, but what I have learned is this: not all my desires will be realized on this side of heaven. However, maybe God has placed me here at such a time as this[1] so I can help meet the needs of those we have neglected.

That missiology project birthed the Parents of Goers ministry. Over the past two years, this ministry has consisted of the Parents of Goers Blog and the Parents of Goers Podcast. It has now expanded to include the book you have in your hand today, *The Missionary Mama's Survival Guide*.

Many of the ups and downs of releasing my son to pursue missions brought to mind the rigors and challenges of a long hike. The journey was scary and confusing, and it was strangely reminiscent of my family's extended hiking trips. Because of these similarities, I have decided to lay out the sending journey as a backpacking adventure. I will be including many of my family's own stories because I think they are apt metaphors for this unfamiliar parenting experience. It is my hope and prayer that they will equip you for the journey ahead.

IT'S NOT A VACATION; IT'S A THRU-HIKE

During the very chilly and rainy May before my fiftieth birthday, my twenty-three-year-old daughter, Tess, and I decided to attempt a thru-hike of the Superior Hiking Trail in northern Minnesota. In case you are unfamiliar with the term, a thru-hike is an end-to-end backpacking trip on a long-distance trail. In this instance, the trail was over 300 miles long, and yes, we slept in a tent.[2]

During our first week on the trail, it rained every single day (and most nights), and the mud nearly sucked our boots off our feet. Being twenty-six years older—and less enthusiastic—than my hiking companion, I could feel my mood becoming as heavy as my drenched backpack. I suggested that we hike into the quaint village of Grand Marais and stay in a hotel. Tess, now nearly hypothermic, agreed. After enjoying hot showers and a large pepperoni pizza, we sat on the bed and discussed our progress thus far. Venting my frustration at the pace that Tess wished to hike, I said, "I want to cut our daily mileage so I can enjoy my vacation." Surprised, and somewhat miffed at her choice of hiking buddy, Tess replied, "Mom, this isn't a vacation! It's a thru-hike!"

My daughter had something to teach me. When I started writing this book, I envisioned it as more of a lament, as in, *"I am lamenting that this journey of having my son overseas isn't more like a vacation."* But after a few weeks of writing and several conversations with God, I decided that this survival guide needed to be more of a pep talk: *"This isn't a vacation! It's a VERY LONG thru-hike"* (but in a much nicer tone than my above-mentioned hiking buddy used). The reason this distinction is important is that a thru-hike is very different from a vacation. A thru-hike takes careful and complicated planning, a tremendous amount of stamina, and prodigious perseverance. A vacation takes planning too, but, at least in theory, it requires much less adrenaline and refreshes you after you have taken it.[3] A thru-hike can only refresh you if you think about it properly. If you prepare yourself for a long and arduous journey rather than a quick and easy change of scenery, then at the end you will be stronger and feel proud of yourself for surviving. If you believe this long journey will be a gentle walk on a level path in flip flops, then you are in for a rude awakening—and maybe some skinned knees.

This Missionary Mama journey is no vacation, and it may take longer than you would like. But it's the road before you, sister, so it's time to stretch out those tentative trail legs and join me on the path.

A CALLING YOU HAVE BEEN GIVEN

You are, or soon will be, living out a calling that you have been given (a thru-hike) and not necessarily the calling you envisioned (a vacation). This calling produces a peculiar sorrow; it is a form of suffering that is very real. And though this suffering is mild in comparison to the suffering of Missionary Mamas of the past (now is NOT the time to read *Foxe's Book of Martyrs*), who had no cell phones, or email, or video chats, it still matters to God. And to me. In this book, I aim not only to share the comfort he has given me but also to offer the courage I have gained by following him.

By walking with God on this hike, I have discovered a spacious place of freedom—a place of acceptance, even joy. I want you to discover it too.

Struggling sister, you are an unsung heroine of The Great Commission. I hope this book is a balm for your soul, a shelter for your spirit, and a safe place for you to lay your burden down. I pray that the words of my mouth and the meditations of my heart will be pleasing not only to you, but to God—our ultimate missionary parent—as well.

> "He brought me out into a spacious place; he rescued me because he delighted in me."
> (Psalm 18:19)

—Tori R. Haverkamp

PART 1
WHERE AM I GOING?

Chapter 1
AN UNFAMILIAR JOURNEY

I have an epileptic dog named Jet. Jet often accompanies me on runs or hikes, so when he was first diagnosed, I was concerned that his new condition would end our adventures together. On the advice of my vet, I decided to medicate him so we could control his unpredictable attacks. About two hours after starting the medication, Jet seemed incredibly unsteady; he missed the corner when following me and ran headlong into the wall. Thinking this strange behavior might be due to the new meds, I called my vet, but he was unavailable. So I did what all modern humans do when we are panic-stricken and need answers NOW. I exclaimed, "Siri, why is my dog acting drunk?"

Siri calmly informed me that "Some dogs struggle with ataxia after starting treatment for seizures. The term ataxia describes a lack of muscle control or coordination of voluntary movements. Ataxia can produce a sense of unsteadiness or weakness. Symptoms of ataxia include poor coordination, a tendency to stumble, and difficulty with fine motor tasks, such as eating, writing, or buttoning a shirt." Though I hadn't witnessed Jet trying to write his name or button his shirt, he had nearly overturned an end table and had slammed his head into the side of my desk. Jet continued to struggle a bit with this foreign unsteadiness in those first few days, but his body soon became accustomed to the stabilizing medicine, and his normal bouncy—and balanced—gait returned.

A DIFFERENT DREAM

When my son and daughter-in-law flew across the ocean just one year after they were married, they were excited for the new adventure that awaited them. I was also excited for them, but the anxiety of the new arrangement seemed to outweigh the joy.

When my son went to church camp as a grade schooler, I felt a similar sense of anxiety from the unknown: Will he be able to sleep in a strange bed? Will he get homesick? Will he need me? I dutifully attended the parent meeting, signed the forms, and read and reread the paperwork assuring me he would be well supervised. Because I had some knowledge of his accommodations, his schedule, and assurance of his safety, I could relax and trust God to take care of him on his week away. But when my little camper became an adult and decided to make his home in a new land, I had the difficult task of reconciling a dream of family togetherness with a process of separation for which I had not been prepared. There was no parent meeting, no paperwork, and no assurance of supervision or safety. I prayed and tried to release him fully to God's care, but my lack of knowledge about where he was going and what he was doing made me feel . . . wobbly.

EMOTIONAL ATAXIA

At first this wobbliness manifested itself in busyness and lack of communication. I filled my life with other activities to try to rebalance my emotional scale, and because of this busyness, I neglected to set a regular time of communication with my Goer, which made me feel even more disconnected from him. I decided to put my feelings of helplessness into a separate emotional "box" that I only took out when I had time to ruminate. As the days wore on, I chided myself for my emotional ataxia and willed myself to "snap out of it"; however, this drill-sergeant-like self-talk did nothing for my balance, and I continued to listlessly participate in my now-unfamiliar life. I regularly struggled with guilt, fear, shame, and confusion. I looked for books, pamphlets, support groups—anything—to help me figure out how to stay close to my far-away family, but I found little to soothe my soul. The resources for parents of missionaries were surprisingly scant, and I realized that these parents, especially the Missionary Mamas like me, were struggling with this unfamiliar journey. The trail seemed so hard to follow, and eventually I decided to create some way-markers to help others navigate the path I had found.

GOD'S KIDS

I didn't use my innate sense of direction or my rad wilderness skills to find a better path; I didn't use my intuition as a guide. Rather, I yoked myself to Jesus, who is gentle and humble in heart, and who gave me rest for my soul.[4] My new life as a Missionary Mama made me feel unsteady, but little by little, I grew sturdier and more secure. By sharing my uncomfortable load with Jesus, I began to surrender a burden that felt heavy and take up a new pack that fits me so much better. By learning about God's mission for the world, accepting my child's vocation, and embracing—instead of resenting—my role as the mom of a missionary, I began to successfully (at least most of the time) survive and thrive.

Maybe you are feeling wobbly about your child's departure. Maybe you don't know what to feel. That's okay. Here's a steadying truth: our Goers are God's kids, and he loves them more than we do! This is mind-blowing but true. And we need to remember that when God invites a son or daughter into missions, he also invites the parents. Will you accept his invitation?

Chapter 2
CHARTING THE PATH

In the summer of 2010, our family of six put our oft-used backpacks inside large duffel bags so they would qualify as checked luggage on our long flight to Alaska. Hiking backpacks are what one might call *unruly*, with a variety of straps, cords, and utensils hanging off the sides. No one likes clanging spoons or excess paracord catching on the airplane seats as they are walking down the aisle. So, we checked these most essential pieces of our gear and traversed the nerve-wracking narrowness with ease. After a long flight and a late lunch, we enjoyed bicycle riding and window shopping in the city of Anchorage.

The following morning, we made our way out of town and drove several hours to Denali National Park. We attended the required "Bear Training"[5] courses at the ranger station (more on this in Chapter 9), recorded our intended itinerary in the park log, and headed out on our big adventure. After hours of bushwhacking side by side through the thick, brushy, and trailless route (Denali has a limited trail network), we were confused about how to find a proper place to pitch our tents. We surveyed our topographical map, but with the absence of established trails (and therefore no way-markers), we ended up wandering around confused in the wilderness for much of our trip.

Even though we had hiked often as a family, we had never backpacked in a place where the route was so undefined. Our wandering was not the result of our own negligence; we wandered aimlessly because we had no established path to follow. (Thankfully, all six of us survived with minimal trauma.)

When your child decides to become a missionary, you may feel a little like you are wandering in the wilderness. Instead of bears, you may find fears, which can feel just as dangerous and daunting. I have been there many times, Mama. The hike has not been easy, but I have learned so much. Will you walk with me as we chart the path before us by learning about God's mission?

MISSIO WHAT?

Learning about the meaning of God's mission can shed light on this strange new path you are on. The phrase *Missio Dei* is Latin for "the mission of God." But what *is* the mission of God? And why is it important? Simply put, the mission of God is to reconcile the whole world back to himself through Jesus Christ. Our God lovingly created a people that wantonly rebelled against him,[6] and ever since that day, he has been acting to draw them close again. The ultimate expression of this was the sending of Jesus, whose death on the cross paid for the people's rebellion and whose resurrection offered them life eternal. The mission of God, then, is to woo these wanderers back into a relationship with himself, and unless people willingly deny themselves and acknowledge Christ as Lord, they will spend eternity separated from him. This is why gospel proclamation is so important. In order to restore his relationship with sinful humanity, God uses his redeemed people as his agents of reconciliation. Sometimes that means he uses our kids.

My child is an agent? Yes, in a way. We call them a variety of things: missionaries, cross-cultural workers, church planters, and, for the purposes of this book, Goers. When my church's global missions department was trying to develop a way to speak of our missionaries discreetly so that we wouldn't draw attention to their activities, we settled on *Goers*, since *Missionary* is a word that is often flagged by hostile governments. God calls all of his people to go with the gospel, and some of them to do so vocationally in another culture, so Goers are an essential part of fulfilling his plan to redeem people from every nation, tribe, people, and language.[7]

MAN'S CHIEF END

The task of our Goers, then, is to introduce others to the mission of God and invite them into it. How do they do this? By glorifying God! The Westminster Shorter Catechism[8] explains:

> Q. What is the chief end of man?
> A. *Man's chief end is to glorify God, and to enjoy him forever.*

As global ambassadors of the one true God, our Goers complete the task placed before them by glorifying God and enjoying him forever. This is a task for all of us, but Goers specifically achieve it by *telling*. When our Goers *speak* the name of Jesus and tell others how to glorify and enjoy him, they are participating in *Missio Dei*. Their individual *end* is to point towards God's glory so that reconciliation between God and his children can happen. Our kids are agents of reconciliation for God. How wondrous!

You see, this *going* business, in which our kids leave their homes and travel across the ocean, isn't about our kids at all.

Or about us.

It's about God.

GOD'S MASTER PLAN

Twelve years ago, when our son was contemplating overseas missions, my husband, our son, and I enrolled in a class called *Perspectives*. For those unfamiliar with the course, *Perspectives on the World Christian Movement* is a course "designed around four vantage points or 'perspectives'—Biblical, Historical, Cultural, and Strategic. Each one highlights different aspects of God's global purpose."[9] In this class, we learned that God's global purpose (*Missio Dei*) is to bring all people—every tongue, tribe, and nation—to himself.[10] As Christians, then, our chief end is to tell others of God's glory and invite them to join the family. In his book *The Mission of God*, Christopher Wright gives a succinct (albeit wordy) definition: Mission is "our committed participation as God's people at God's invitation and command, in God's own mission within the history of the world for the redemption of God's creation."[11]

The *Perspectives* class and other books (such as Wright's) helped me and my future Goer grasp the big picture of missions; it was not to be understood just as the expansion of Christianity globally, but rather as the task given to Christ-followers everywhere to "communicate the good news not only with their words but also with their lives and deeds."[12] We are *all* to live as people on mission, joining God in what he is already doing to redeem his people and his creation. Mission is God's idea. It's not the church's or the missions organization's invention. And I don't have to know every detail of my kids' daily lives to understand their job; their task is the same as mine, just in a different culture. We are supposed to live our lives in a way that brings glory to God and makes him attractive to the world.

Because I had already begun to grasp God's grand intention, when our son announced his decision to serve overseas, I was mentally able to process the "why" of his departure with relative ease.

My emotions, however, didn't get the memo.

Maybe yours didn't, either. Your feelings, like mine, may be loud and in your face, but track with me, sister, and you will be able to train them to keep in step with the truth. By doing this, you will have the strength to resist self-pity during anxious times ahead. Rehearsing the purpose and importance of missions will help you focus on your child's calling and on God's amazing compassion.

TO THE DOUBTING MAMA

Hopefully, the cheery pep talk I just gave sounds inspirational to believers. If I were not a Christ-follower, though, I think I would be skeptical of anyone who claimed to know God's purpose for the world. You might be a parent who thinks your Goer is too religious, too serious, and too far away from home. You may resent this whole "Master Plan"—and maybe even God himself, who seems to be the one responsible for your child's absence.

I wish I could invite you over for coffee and talk with you about Jesus. I wish I could show you that he is faithful and strong and true. But since I can't, please let me say this: God created us to reflect him, but we humans do this so imperfectly. So, in his abundant grace, he sent Jesus to be perfect for us. When we put our trust in this sinless Savior, he takes the burden of our sin and shows us a path of glory that truly leads us home. This is the gospel. Your kids are not abandoning you. They believe the gospel and want others to believe it too. Ask them about their relationship with Jesus, about the people they serve, about their hopes for the future. And keep on loving them—even if you don't fully understand—as they pursue God's mission for the world. Stick with me, Missionary Mama. It's always better to hike with a buddy.

A school assignment completed by my future missionary at age six.

PART 2
HOW WILL I GET THERE?

Chapter 3
LEARNING THE LINGO

When discussing adventures, our family refers to three kinds of fun: Type 1, Type 2, and Type 3.[13] Since these terms may be unfamiliar to you, allow me to explain.

> » **Type 1 fun** – Fun to do, and fun to remember
> » **Type 2 fun** – Not fun to do, but fun to remember
> » **Type 3 fun** – Not fun to do, and not fun to remember

When my son, who apparently decided he wanted to become a mishinainae[14] in kindergarten, finally became a Goer, it seemed to me that he was experiencing Type 1 and Type 2 fun. I was solidly in Type 3; I was not having fun being the mom of a Goer. I was anxious and fearful—even angry that he was making my life inconvenient—and I was experiencing his departure as painful. Memories that should have brought me joy, like recalling past birthdays or inside jokes that we shared, only served to remind me of all I had lost by having him so far away.

As I began to trace his steps—from his first *mishinainae* declaration, to his childhood obsession with maps, to his early short-term mission trips—I began to see that it was not only the adventure that was pulling him towards the mission lifestyle, but it was ultimately his understanding of God's call upon his life. My son wasn't leaving me to pursue Type 1 and 2 fun; he was being obedient to what God had shown him. Now my job was to learn as much as I could about that choice so I could push on to Type 1 and Type 2 fun myself and leave Type 3 behind.

To help me run towards Type 1 fun, I looked up all the missions words I didn't know. Like any other subculture, missionaries have their own lingo. Some of this is a result of their unique calling: unique jobs have a unique vocabulary. Some of it grew out of the need to use safe words in countries that weren't Christian-friendly.

And what about Type 2 fun? Did I run towards that as well? Running towards 2 wasn't required because, with a proper perspective of my child's role, I can view almost all of life as Type 2. Some things in this life—like being a world away from your loved ones—are not fun in the moment, but oh how delightful it will be to remember and giggle about them together in heaven! God promises a special reward for our peculiar sorrow: "Truly I tell you, no one who has left home or wife or brothers or sisters or parents or children for the sake of the kingdom of God will fail to receive many times as much in this age, and in the age to come eternal life" (Luke 18:29-30). So now, without further ado, let's sprint towards Type 1 with gusto!

FROM THE MOUTHS OF MISSIONARY BABES

Prepare yourself. This is a really long, but incredibly helpful, list. It will help you know what I'm talking about if you happen to spy these words in future chapters. As an added bonus, it will also provide you with a little more "street cred" as you hang with your kids during those cryptic video-call sessions.

» Missionary/Goer/Cross-Cultural Worker: This is what your child is right now. He/she has chosen to go and live cross-culturally to take God's message of reconciliation—his mission—to the world.

» Stayer: This is you. They, the Goers, have gone away; you have stayed behind. That is the hard part of this whole adventure.

» The Great Commission: The Great Commission, which is recorded in Matthew 28:18–20, was spoken by Jesus to his disciples as he sent them out to make disciples in his name: "Then Jesus came to them and said, 'All authority in heaven and on earth has been given to me. Therefore go and make disciples of all nations, baptizing them in the name of the Father and of the Son and of the Holy Spirit, and teaching them to obey everything I have commanded you. And surely I am with you always, to the very end of the age.'" This commission is not only for the ancient disciples; it's for us too! Our kids are seeking to obey the Great Commission when they "go."

» Proselytization/Evangelism: While these words have similar meanings, they are not exactly the same. Proselytization has a more negative connotation. It conjures up images of the Crusades, where mostly non-interested parties were talked at and forced to convert to the Christian faith. In contrast, evangelism is a two-way conversation between your child and a new acquaintance. In this conversation, your child will try to gain trust from this person by talking with them in the hope of sharing Jesus in a loving way. Proselytizing is illegal in certain cultures, while evangelizing is sometimes allowed. However, both of these activities are frowned upon in some countries.

» Creative Access (formerly Closed or Limited Access) Nation: In the past the terms "closed" and "limited" access were used to describe countries where traditional missionary activity was illegal or banned. Most missions thinkers today now utilize the term "creative access nation" instead. This more commonly applied term acknowledges that while there are countries that are closed to traditional missionary ministry, they are not really closed to the gospel.[15] In creative access countries, our kids use their vocation (see this term below) to do CAM (Creative Access Missions) to serve God.

» Visa/Visa Run: A visa is a document your kids need in order to be in their country of service. A visa must be applied for and then approved by the government. This process is not always simple. Many Goers can't list their true reason for wanting to be in a country, so they have to apply for a student visa (and then become a student), a work visa (if they have a small business), or even a tourist visa. Tourist visas usually have to be renewed at regular intervals (often every ninety days) by leaving the country and coming back into it as a "tourist." When your Goer has this type of visa, they will need to cross an international border just so they can re-enter their country of residence as a tourist and reset their visa. We call that process a visa run. If you go to visit your child, you will need a tourist visa as well. Most likely you will stay less than ninety days, so no visa run for you.

» Vocation: Vocation is how each individual person uses their unique strengths and gifts to contribute to the good of the world. Each of us has interests and passions that can propel us forward in service and creativity. When Christians faithfully complete the work God brings to them, they are fulfilling God's purpose for their lives. Our vocation may be teacher, homemaker, healthcare worker, pastry chef, or grandkid-spoiler. Our kids call what they do their vocation, and it may involve being a church planter, a student, a professional, a healthcare worker, or a translator.

» Church Planter: What is this business called church planting? A church planter is a person who desires to see God's church flourish throughout the world. Our kids "plant" churches by introducing people to Jesus, inviting them to be part of a local body of believers, providing them with loving discipleship and adequate instruction so they might grow in the faith, and helping raise up church leaders from the local culture.

» Student: We are all familiar with this term. It means "a person who goes to school." For our kids, it may mean "a person who goes to school even when they already have a degree (or two)." When trying to obtain a visa for residency in a creative access country, your child will need to declare their reason for being there. When outright proselytizing is forbidden in a place, our Goers have to be more creative in living out their vocations, so some of them go back to school. Some of them also become teachers, which is a type of BAM (see below).

»BAM: This onomatopoeia-like acronym stands for Business as Mission. Jo Plummer writes, "Business is a God-given vocation and institution in society, with the potential to bring multiple benefits to people, communities and nations. Business as Mission intentionally leverages this intrinsic power of business to address spiritual needs, hand in hand with social, economic and environmental needs."[16] BAM is sometimes referred to as kingdom business, missional entrepreneurship, transformational business, or missional business. If your child checked "professional" on his/her visa, then they are most likely participating in BAM.

» Translator: A translator is a person who translates one language into another. Some of our kids will apply to be a translator and then work for a school, a camp, or a business. Their job is to make the speaker's words and ideas understandable to the listener's ear.

» Platform/Tentmaking: A platform is your child's job in the area of medicine, education, or business, among others. These jobs allow government-approved access to places where missionaries cannot enter. Another term that you may hear is "tentmaking," which comes from Acts 18:3 and describes how the apostle Paul supported himself by making tents while living and preaching in Corinth. Tentmaking missionaries do some kind of work in their country of service to financially support themselves.

» NGO: This stands for Non-Governmental Organization. An NGO is a nonprofit organization that operates independently of any government, typically with the purpose of addressing a social or political issue.

» Fellowship/ Club/ Gathering/ House Group: When our kids lived in a culture with a government that was hostile towards Christians, they often held their church services in people's homes or apartments. Since they didn't want to be flagged by officials for participating in these weekly meetings, they refrained from calling them "churches." Instead, they chose *the* *word club* when they communicated with others. Other teams may call their meetings *fellowships*, or something humorous like *the circus*. When you are talking to them about this, be intentional about referring to their churches in this way.

» Safe Language: As mentioned previously, some of the countries where our kids live frown upon Christianity and anything that sounds like it might have something to do with Christianity. It is for this reason that many of us must make a concerted effort to employ safe language when talking to our kids.[17] Some governments target certain words in written or spoken communication (over internet or phone) to try to locate missionaries (who are people of interest to them). Don't ask your kids for tips on this unless you are with them in person, just in case their communication with you is being monitored. Here are some common shortened or symbolic replacements for common Christian vocabulary (valid with caps or no caps):

> **God:** the Father, G_d, g@d, Dad
> **Jesus:** the Son
> **Holy Spirit:** HS
> **Pray:** yarp, pr@y, ask, lift
> **Missionary:** M, worker
> **Baptism:** Dunk, getting dunked
> **Evangelize:** EV, fishing
> **Church:** Club, Sunday gathering
> **Fellow Christians:** family, brothers and sisters

» Culture Shock: Culture shock is the feeling of disorientation experienced by someone who is subjected to an unfamiliar culture, way of life, or set of attitudes. When your kids go on the field, this disorientation may happen suddenly and make them long for home. Don't rescue them from this—or from other "spiritual muscle building" experiences—by encouraging them to come home. Go ahead and sympathize, but stop before your natural parental protection response kicks in. It is all part of the process of becoming an effective ambassador for God in a foreign land. Culture shock may also happen in a reverse sort of way when they come back to the States to visit because they will have (hopefully) acclimated to their host culture by that time.

» **Acclimation:** Acclimation is the process of becoming accustomed to a new culture or to new conditions. When your kids first go abroad, their missions organization will likely limit their visits home for the first eighteen months to two years to help them become fully acclimated to their new homes. Don't complain about this; it is a difficult but very necessary part of the process.

» **Incarnational Living:** This one is a little harder to explain, but I will give it a try. When our kids talk about incarnational living, they are referring to the way Jesus lived among us when he came to earth. John 1:14 describes it like this: "The Word became flesh and made his dwelling among us." In Greek, this passage literally reads, "the Word became flesh and pitched his tent among us."[18] (How appropriate for a backpacking-themed book!) As Eugene Peterson puts it, "The Word became flesh and blood, and moved into the neighborhood."[19] God "tented" with the Israelites in the wilderness, and in Christ, God pitches his tent with us. Let me expand on that: Jesus didn't enter the world as a powerful ruler (even though he is); he was born as a baby and allowed himself to endure human hunger, emotions, and pain. He chose to come live among us and be like us so that we could understand what God is like. In a similar way, our kids are going to a foreign culture and trying to become as much like the people they are serving as possible. They don't want to live in their new homes like Americans because they are no longer living in America. They want to love the people around them by living like them, dressing like them, eating like them, and even talking like them. Don't get frustrated if you see your child living differently than they would here at home. Incarnational living is an important and powerful part of their vocation.

» **Passport Country:** Your passport country is the place where you are originally from—the country that issued your passport to you. This is what we are referring to when we say "home." However, there may come a time when your child calls their new culture home and refers to their old home as their passport country. This is sometimes sad for us, but it is a good sign that they have acclimated to their new culture.

» **Host Country:** The host country is the place that is hosting you. In our kids' case, it is also where they serve cross-culturally. Often after living in their service country for several years, they think of it not as their host, but as their home (see above).

» **Support Raising:** Am I the only one who feels sheepish about this part of my child's job? When my son asks my friends and family members for money, it makes me uncomfortable. So how should I think about this very necessary task? Support raising is the way most missionaries "earn a salary" and cover their living and ministry expenses.[20] To try and gain more clarity on this topic, I interviewed the Missions Pastor at our church. Here is what he said: "The main reason that our Goers don't receive a salary from a church is that they are not employed by a church. American pastors and church staff are a part of a cultural context in which there are enough existing Christians to form churches and to support the local staff team. As missionaries step into new cultures, they are in a non-Christian context where there are few or no Christians. Since non-Christians rarely give to the work of missions, the workers need to be supported by Christians in the culture they come from so they can minister to the culture where they are going."[21]

» Mobilization Agency/Missions Organization: These organizations work in cooperation with the local church to "engage, equip, and connect believers worldwide to their most strategic role in the Great Commission."[22] Their mission is to point those who know and follow Jesus to those with no access to the gospel. In layman's terms, they help churches send missionaries, and then they help those missionaries navigate their new lives in their country of service. Missionaries' financial support often gets funneled through the missions organization for tax purposes.

» Sending/Supporting Church: The specific local church that sends missionaries abroad is called the sending or supporting church.[23] In most cases, the sending church is the church that the goers attended before leaving the States. The relationship between the missionary and the sending church is important because it provides a "tether" for both parties. This tether helps the goer feel connected to an authority source and helps stateside believers support the work God is accomplishing through their missionaries.

» Furlough/Home Assignment/Home Service: The official definition of "furlough" is a leave of absence. Home assignment/Home service is a period of weeks or months during which missionaries visit their passport countries. Hypothetically, this period allows sending/supporting churches to reconnect with them and allows the missionaries to recharge before returning to cross-cultural service. The terms above are mostly interchangeable. When your kids leave their country of service for a time, that break is called going on furlough or going on home assignment (which is really a misnomer, since by this time they have usually begun calling their passport country "home"). Sometimes global emergencies force them to take a furlough for an indefinite period. This unique scenario can be frustrating to both the Goers and the Stayers. More on that later.

Whew! You made it. I'm a word girl, so that was definitely Type 1 fun for me. Regardless of the type of fun you are experiencing right now, learning the "Goer lingo" will help keep you in the know. And being in the know makes this new journey a whole lot easier.

Chapter 4
TRAINING FOR THE TRAIL

A few years after my husband, Brent, and I became empty nesters, we decided to take a backpacking trip sans children. We had never done this before. I guess we somehow assumed that our adventures had to include six hikers; this time we realized we could do it differently and decided to try the trail with two. On our previous hiking trips, I had a variety of people to talk to, sing with, and rely on when I felt unmotivated. Someone always hiked with me when the hills were steep or the miles seemed long. This time, however, after just a couple of miles, my hubby turned around and said, "You're too slow. I'm going to go on ahead." I faintly protested, knowing that I *was* slow, and yelled after him pitifully, "What if I can't find the trail?" He hollered as he sped away, "Just follow the cairns[24] and you'll be fine."

Fine, yes; happy, no.

In that moment I was unhappy because I had really wanted someone to hike with me. And sometimes being unhappy is par for the course—things in life are bound to upset us. But while being unhappy is okay, it's important that we don't let our unhappiness pull us into sinful thought patterns.

THE COLOR OF EMOTIONS

Unhappiness is not the problem. Emotions are not the problem. Emotions are the God-given GPS system for our bodies. They provide depth, insight, and imagination to our brains. If our brains provide the outline for understanding our circumstances, then our emotions fill in that outline with vibrant color. In the Old Testament, we see God displaying a range of different emotions, including feelings of love, jealousy, and joy (Jer. 31:3; Exod. 20:5; Zeph. 3:17). Jeremiah powerfully laments the destruction of Jerusalem in Lamentations, and David's deep emotions populate the book of Psalms. In the New Testament, Jesus shows compassion (Matt 9:36), delight (Luke 10:21), sadness (Luke 19:41), and empathy (John 19:26–27). Peter shows impulsiveness (Luke 22:33), and James and John are nicknamed "Sons of Thunder" (Mark 3:17), probably for good reason.

The Bible is composed of a variety of stories of real people with real emotions. God even shows us that *he* has emotions—after all, he is the one who created them. So, emotions are not the problem on our Missionary Mama hike, although the misuse of them can be. When we choose to let our emotions run amok, we are not taking every thought captive. Training yourself for this journey requires the training of your emotions.

TAKE EVERY THOUGHT CAPTIVE

Remember my lonely hiking day? I didn't take my thoughts captive that day. My emotional training was lax and lazy. As I walked alone, I let my feelings climb a self-righteous stairway of judgment. I deemed myself superior and my husband inept. In my state of unhappiness, I didn't resist the devil as he deftly decanted the acid of resentment towards Brent into my mind:

"Who does he think he is?"
"He doesn't really love you."
"If he loved you well, then he would never leave you alone."
"He is a bad leader for you."

When Brent went on ahead, he did it simply because he enjoys hiking alone and his pace is faster than mine. There was no evil intent in his heart. He did not wish to harm me. Nor did any of these things even enter his mind. He has long legs and takes one step for every three of mine.

However, I chose to believe the wrong story. I assumed the worst in him rather than thinking the best of him. I cozied up to my sinful, self-focused emotions, pulled them around me like a fuzzy blanket, and cried alligator tears as I plodded along the trail looking for the infamous cairns.

Sisters, this was the wrong way to handle my disappointment. There is a very good reason that Paul admonishes his readers in 2 Corinthians 10:5 to "demolish arguments and every pretension that sets itself up against the knowledge of God, and . . . take captive every thought to make it obedient to Christ." Demolish. Captive. Obedient. Them's some strong words, fellow Mamas. The reason God instructs us to walk in a certain way is that it brings us *life*. To experience the abundance that he wants to breathe into our lives, we have to demolish wrong thoughts and recognize faulty thinking patterns; we have to take them *captive*. To be fully alive, we must choose obedience to God's way rather than defaulting to our natural, self-protective, fuzzy-blanket emotions. We do this by learning how to filter our thoughts.

FILTERING OUT IMPURITIES

When my family goes backpacking nowadays, we purify the water we get from streams, rivers, and lakes by using a SteriPen. A SteriPen is a hand-held device that can be dipped into a water bottle to sterilize the water. This nifty device uses ultraviolet (UV) light waves to disrupt the DNA within bacteria, viruses, and protozoa. The process renders them unable to reproduce little baby bacterias. This is happy news when the lake you are camping beside is teeming with tiny worms that, when ingested, can produce cysts in your liver and lungs. Although this device kills harmful bacteria and other bugs, it does not *filter out* those things. The water pump we used to carry (which we discarded because it was tedious to use) used a carbon filter with a little sieve attached. This water purifying method strained out *both* the impurities and the gross after-effects. Not so with the SteriPen. When we see the tiny dead things floating in our drinking water, we either pour our water through our bandanas to strain it (super high tech), or we just close our eyes and drink it.

When we become Christians, we receive the gift of the Holy Spirit, and with that Spirit gift, the capacity for a transformed mind. Paul instructs new believers in Rome to resist the temptation to approve the pagan mores of Roman culture. And in Romans 12:2, he encourages them to "be transformed by the renewing of your mind. Then you will be able to test and approve what God's will is—his good, pleasing and perfect will." If we are to renew our mind for the journey ahead, we must transform it by removing the impurities from our thought patterns. Our brains can perform like SteriPens when we use them within our natural power; we can *will* ourselves to think with truth, but the gross after-effect of sin means that we will still have pieces and parts of that faulty thinking hanging around to haunt us. When we receive the gift of God's Spirit, we have the ability not only to *purify* our thoughts but also to *disarm* and *remove* the nasty gnats of deception that Satan uses to trick us.

Thinking with our renewed mind is like using the old-school water purification system, but better. It might take a little longer to use. It may be a lot more tedious. But it's worth the extra time and effort to get the "Living Water" (see John 4) that allows us to hydrate our spirits with God's pleasing, perfect will and to fill our mind with filtered (and de-bugged) thoughts.

FAULTY THINKING

In her extraordinarily helpful book *The Emotionally Healthy Woman*, Geri Scazzero labels the type of thinking that I employed on my "Brent is bad" hike as **faulty thinking**. She proposes that "Faulty thinking is a deadly threat to emotional and spiritual health. It can:

- » mire you in powerlessness
- » paralyze you in hopelessness
- » cut you off from joyful living
- » lock you up in unnecessary pain

She goes on to say, "It's also contagious and can spread to

other areas of your life. This makes faulty thinking even more dangerous because it operates, for the most part, beyond our conscious awareness. Eradicating this deadly disease requires such radical surgery that it can almost be compared to getting a brain transplant!"[25]

Short of having a brain transplant, how can we train ourselves to nix this faulty thinking? First, as we have on the journey thus far, we must define the problem:

> » **"Where are we going?"** In this faulty thinking scenario, we are going wherever our minds want to take us. We have to decide to go somewhere else.
> » **"How will we get there?"** We get there by changing our default way of processing emotions. We do this by filtering our thoughts.
> » **"What do we do now?"** We get to work!

Scazzero explains more of this process:

> In [faulty thinking] scenarios, the problem arises when feelings from the past hijack clear thinking in the present. Our feelings have been so hardwired that they override our logical thought process. Overwhelming feelings prevent us from asking clarifying questions: What is going on here? What are the facts? What do I know to be true? God has given us an inner guidance system to move through life—thinking and feeling. It is essential that we pay attention to our feelings. But then we must think about what to do with them. Knowing when to follow our feelings and when not to is indispensable if we are to grow up into spiritual adulthood in Christ.[26]

Let me repeat: "Overwhelming feelings prevent us from asking clarifying questions." Is this true for you, Missionary Mama? Maybe you're not doing any internal husband-bashing, but are you thinking rightly about your child's vocation? Are you even thinking about how you are thinking?

Maybe some of you have quieter emotions than I had. Or perhaps you've been able to line up your thoughts in your mind and sweetly ask them to obey the truth. I was unable to do that. To change my faulty thinking, I had to practice something akin to lion training. In this scenario my large emotions lumber around the arena, roaring to be fed with juicy tidbits, while I stand by feebly, intimidated by their hugeness and their power. To take them "captive," I have to get the whip of wisdom, snap it a few times in their presence, and get to work on making them obey Christ.

FILTERED THINKING

This emotional workout would be what Scazzero refers to as **accurate thinking**. For the purposes of our book, we will call this exercise **filtered thinking**. To be able to think accurately, we must *filter* our thoughts through the sieve of God's truth. When a way of thinking or acting is deeply ingrained, it will take more than a mere decision to change it. You will need a plan.

My plan is simple: I expose the lie by speaking the truth (*faulty* vs *filtered*). When I catch myself in faulty thinking about my Goer (or anything else) and manage to battle my roaring emotions to the ground, I say this out loud:

"This is the lie," and I list my faulty thinking.

"This is the truth," and I remind myself of how to think by using my renewed mind.

When I don't allow my emotions to control me, I can think with truth. Emotions are appropriate and helpful when they lead me towards wholeness and joy. Emotions are bad guides when they make me focus on myself. When I walk in wisdom, switching from faulty thinking to filtered thinking can happen with just a choice, but sometimes my strong feelings make that switch muddier than I'd like. It might be the same for you.

Just for fun, let's practice switching our thinking with some of my own faulty thoughts:

FAULTY THINKING	FILTERED THINKING
My Goer is leaving because he doesn't love me.	He does love me! His departure is not a sign of rejection, but of obedience to God.
No one cares about my pain.	God cares about my pain. He understands when I miss my child. And other Missionary Mamas understand. I can ask them to pray for me.
I will always feel the grief I feel now.	My grief may not go away completely, but it will feel less intense with time, education, and God's faithful love.
Our relationship will never be the same.	If I intentionally reach out, we can still be close.
I will not be able to enjoy family times without my child.	Family may not feel the same, but I can choose to enjoy the life God is giving me now while also looking forward to his future visits.
What if he needs me and I can't get there quickly?	I must surrender him to God. His team is caring for him. If I really need to make a trip, I can.

If you are struggling to think rightly about your new life with your Goer abroad, then grab some friends, tell them what you have learned about faulty thinking and filtered thinking, and ask them to call you out when you start down an unhealthy path. Start your own chart like mine and begin practicing the switch from faulty to filtered.

This is how you do it: get on your knees and ask God to show you the ways your emotions may be leading you astray. Pray that he would renew your mind so that you will be able to recognize faulty thoughts. Then capture these thoughts and make them obedient to Christ. Repeat as often as you need.

Hang in there, sister. Training your mind for the trail ahead takes practice, but it doesn't require perfection. That's what Jesus is for.

Chapter 5
FOLLOWING THE CAIRNS

I have spoken previously about my epileptic dog, Jet. This story is not about him. It's about the dog that preceded him. That dog's name was Neo.

When Neo was entering his senior years, we thought it would be a nice last hurrah for him to go with us on a family backpacking trip. He had been on several trips with us before and had always enjoyed the beautiful outdoors, the intense family time, and the all-day-long walks. Neo had always been a perfect gentledog on the trail and at the campsites (with the one exception of when he ate an entire one-pound block of cheese). Though he had gained some weight lately, he seemed to be frisky enough to join us.

On the first day of the hike, he carried his girth well and trotted contentedly behind the family. On the second day, his pace slowed a bit. On the third day, Neo stopped to rest at every shade tree and plopped his hot self into every puddle on the trail. Eventually, he stopped altogether.

When he refused to start again, we came up with a plan. We grabbed the salami log that we had been slowly working through during mealtimes and started cutting off tiny slices and laying them on the trail. Then we pulled the dog towards the first enticing chunk and allowed him to sniff its tantalizing aroma.

With minimal coaching, Neo ate the initial chunk and moved forward towards another. Little by little, salami chunk by salami chunk, he made his way to our campsite. It was a long process, but it achieved the goal of successfully bringing him to our stopping place.

A BETTER PATH

Remember in the last chapter when I talked about "faulty thinking"? In the above scenario, Neo decided that he couldn't go any further. This was the canine version of faulty thinking. To help him filter his thinking, we made a trail of salami. Since dogs have no ability to "capture their thoughts," we helped Neo find a better path by giving him "markers" to follow (and eat!).

Remember when Brent told me to "Just follow the cairns and you'll be fine"? It was his way of leaving a little salami trail for me. Though he didn't place the cairns, he advised me to look for some (non-edible) ancient way-markers so I could stay on the right trail and not get lost. He was taking care of me, even though I was convinced he didn't care. But that's what faulty thinking does. It leads you in the wrong mental direction—and speedily.

WHAT IN THE WORLD IS A CAIRN?

Cairn (pronounced exactly like it looks—kind of a quick "*Kar-*

en") is a Scottish term for a man-made pile or stack of stones. Cairns are used all over the world as landmarks and are specifically used as trail markers on many hiking paths.

When my husband told me to follow these markers, he was giving me general directions for how to stay on the right trail. I followed his advice, and a few hours later, we met at our agreed-upon destination. Even though it wasn't my favorite hiking day, I was able to find the cairns and keep walking. But the whole journey would have been better if I had realized my faulty thinking and replaced it with truth. That didn't happen that day, but it has happened since. God, a gracious and patient Schoolmaster, has taught me so much about himself—and myself—during my times of struggle.

In my effort to be a good survival guide, I am highlighting the cairns that have been the most helpful on my Missionary Mama journey. I hope they will help you stay on the path as well.

THE CAIRN OF GRATITUDE

»The Cairn of Gratitude helps you see what is good.«

Now is the time to count your blessings, sister. Instead of ruminating on everything that you don't like about this new way of life, look for the ways you are blessed. When I was really struggling after my son went overseas, especially during that very first year, I chose to keep a blessings book to help train my brain with the truth. I wrote down three blessings (or more) that I experienced each day (e.g., *a red cardinal, my husband cleaning up his socks, a warm and cozy bed*). This didn't necessarily remedy my sadness, but it made me feel better about my life in general.

Maybe you're not a journal keeper. That's okay. Make it a point to notice God's common grace, even in your most ordinary moments, and then speak your observations out loud. Instead of complaining when others inquire, smile and tell them what is (truthfully, honestly) good about your new normal. Having an attitude of gratitude will "rewire" your brain so you can develop healthy, rather than fearful or guilt-filled, thought patterns. John Ortberg says it well: "Gratitude is the ability to experience life as a gift. It liberates us from the prison of self-preoccupation."[27]

THE CAIRN OF SURRENDER

»The Cairn of Surrender helps you let go.«

I was once part of a team that traveled to Africa to teach theology to indigenous pastors and their wives. As I spent time with the African women, I became amazed by their ability to do anything—tend a garden, make a meal, catch a chicken—with a baby tied to their back. It was an ingenious solution, and I applauded the women for their creative methods of keeping their children close.

When my son left to go abroad, I remembered those tied-to-mama babies. By tying their babies to their backs, the African women maintained a sense of control. But, as the children grew and became too heavy, the mothers had to untie the knot and release them. Isn't this an apt description of parenting? When our kids are under our roof, we feel we can control their safety. When they fly across the ocean, we forfeit that security. It can make us feel out of control. And we are. But we have never really been in control anyway, because our kids aren't really *our* kids; they're God's.

One of the most important cairns on the trail is surrender. Missionary Mama, when you surrender your kids to live out their vocations, they will develop their own "trail legs" to traverse the specific journey on which God is leading *them*. Notice I said *them*. God is leading your child on a different path than the one you are on, and when you surrender her to God's care (as opposed to your hovering presence), she will develop "spiritual muscles" by leaning on her new-found independence, her developing abilities, her faithful teammates, and her sovereign God. When our kids find themselves in an unfamiliar place, they are more likely to run toward God simply because we are not physically available. This is as it should be, even if it makes us feel less needed. Our kids need to know that we know they can thrive in their new home.

Don't be ashamed or alarmed if this act of surrender makes you feel sad. It's okay to feel that way. When our compass shifts from "hands-on parent" to "coach from afar," we may feel disoriented enough to run to God ourselves.

Your kids are trusting in God's providence and protection. Are you?

THE CAIRN OF FREEDOM

»The Cairn of Freedom leads you towards contentment.«

One cannot find the cairn of freedom without first passing the cairns of gratitude and surrender. When we choose to see what's good in our lives rather than focusing on the lack, and when we give up our tight-fisted grip on our kids' lives, we enter into a restful state of freedom.

Freedom *doesn't* mean your life is free of fear or pain; freedom means that you are not *controlled* by fear or pain. Paul Tripp says, "We invest an amazing amount of time and energy examining how we feel and how we feel about how we feel in comparison to how we are told we should normally feel."[28] How true is that?! As I said before, it's okay for you to struggle with this change, to be "Fine, yes. Happy, no." Life is like that sometimes. But we don't want to let that struggle lead us to faulty thinking, because faulty thinking leads us to sin. And sin can lead us into emotional bondage—a place where we risk getting trapped by our fearful thoughts.

As someone once wisely observed, "Freedom is not the right to do what we want, but what we ought."[29] To do what we ought, we must tell ourselves the right story not only about our situation, but also about our child's vocation.

When you tell yourself what is true about your Goer, you have the *freedom* to think accurately about why your child has chosen to go. He is not rejecting you; he is obeying God. So be his cheerleader, not his critic. When you tell yourself the right story, you have the *freedom to* encourage your child, even when you feel a bit discouraged yourself. Freedom releases us to be in control when our emotions threaten to push us toward the "woe is me" camp.

Conversely, when your child is struggling and it breaks your mama heart, first pause, then pray. (A latte and a little dark chocolate might be good here too.) Walking in truth gives you *freedom from* panic and obsessive thoughts. You may not have the ability to squelch the "rescue urge," but you *do* have the ability to ask God to do the rescuing for you. He is good at that, after all. This kind of freedom, the *freedom from*, will empower you to resist panicking when your Goer doesn't text you back instantaneously (they're probably on the subway). This kind of freedom helps you think with accurate thoughts. Accurate thinking gives you the ability to do what you know you should do: trust God, even when it's hard.

And let's face it: this whole journey is hard. That's why we are hiking it together.

To close, here's a little ditty (written about Neo, the salami-loving dog) to add to your cairn collection. This has absolutely no purpose except to give you a little chuckle.

MY DOG IS FAT

I took my dog to the vet today,
complaining he didn't want to run or play.
The dog seemed lethargic and lazy, I said,
not chasing squirrels, but sleeping instead.
The vet did examine, observe, and explain,
saying the dog's neither sick nor in pain.
He took me aside, his voice very flat,
and said, "Nothing's wrong, miss. Your dog is just fat."

But fat dogs can still make the journey, so let's continue on.

PART 3
WHY IS THIS SO HARD?

Chapter 6
HOT SPOTS AND BLISTERS

My Goer was always fascinated by geography. When he was three, I made him a blanket with a world map on one side and red flannel on the other; by early elementary, he had memorized the locations and names of all of the continents and most of the countries displayed on this map. When he claimed his own room in the basement at thirteen, he convinced me to help him hang a floor-to-ceiling map mural on one wall. (Pro tip: never wallpaper with your teenage son.) By high school, he was wowing his peers by biting his sandwiches into the shapes of most of the states in the U.S. (Hawaii and Michigan are hard), and by his junior year in college, he had spent one entire summer and part of another in a country across the ocean.

When he approached his father and me a few months after his college graduation and told us he felt called to be an overseas missionary, the desire seemed par for the course. Throughout his college career, our son diligently studied foreign languages, interned in his church's global department, and coordinated various international student ministries. As his mind formulated a plan for a missionary life, his heart longed for a missions-loving wife. Then a sweet and spunky girl joined him in the leadership of the International Friendship Connection (IFC) family group he hosted, and he was smitten.

She returned the feeling, and they were married in a matter of months. Nearly a year later, following countless hours of language learning, cross-cultural acclimation courses, and grueling evaluations with their missions agency, they were commissioned by their local church to go abroad. Finally, our son and his new bride took a very long flight across the ocean and made their home in a foreign land.

And on his next birthday, I cried. A lot. Ever since my son went overseas, special days have been hot spots for me.

HOT SPOTS

The initial grieving experience can feel long and overwhelming, but then life begins to fall into a rhythm. Even in our new rhythms and routines, however, we can still experience "hot spots" of grief during certain circumstances or at specific times of year.

Physical hot spots are red, tender areas on the skin that appear before the formation of blisters; they tend to occur on pressure points and chafe points. To avoid hot spots when hiking, one must pay very close attention to their feet and to any other area of possible chafing. Hot spots can make a hiker miserable unless they're addressed immediately upon discovery.

Emotional hot spots can be a regular annoyance on the Missionary Mama journey. These tender areas of your feelings can be rubbed raw when you expect special days, birthdays, and holidays to feel the same without your Goer present. They won't feel the same, and it is a bummer. But just knowing about this disappointment in advance can help you bolster yourself for when your neighbor talks about having "all my chicks together under one roof," or when your sister posts about making valentines with her granddaughter (just when you are aching for your little far-away Valentine). Mentally preparing yourself ahead of time will help when you receive those Christmas cards showing your friends with their fully intact and physically present families.

You will need to remedy those hot spots with immediate action: grab a friend and talk about it. In their book, *Parents of Missionaries*, Cheryl Savageau and Diane Stortz suggest you take full advantage of your friend's listening ear: "Social support helps the grieving process because it gives permission for painful emotions to exist. Support allows us to spend time in a transitional place, doing the work needed to move from our pre-loss state to the new beginnings we must make."[30] Sometimes we want to pull ourselves from the molasses river of grief as quickly as possible, but God's healing timeline isn't always like that. So slow down, Mama. Your hot spot might stay red, but if you put on some cozy socks and attempt an easy-mileage day, you will stave off the blister, and the healing can begin.

Are your friends busy right now? If so, then write a sweet note to your Goer, take a walk in the woods with your dog, or go back to your blessings book. Now is the time to do something to alleviate sadness. Don't wallow in it. Wallowing ignores the problem, and ignored hot spots will soon become blisters.

BLISTERS

If a hiker doesn't address a hot spot, then it will most definitely develop into a blister. A *physical* blister is a fluid-filled space between the layers of the skin—ouch! These seemingly small injuries can cause immense pain, especially if not cared for properly.

An **emotional blister**—I sometimes call it a **heart blister**—results when we Missionary Mamas don't deal with our emotional hot spots. As competent adults, we can choose how we will make sense of our feeling of loss. We can choose what we believe about life. When we choose to believe the wrong things, when we let our sadness pull us into self-absorption, we develop "blisters on our hearts." Heart blisters can cause us to be perpetually unhappy and resentful. Heart blisters can make us mad about our Goer's absence. They can even make us mad at our Goer.

Both physical blisters and heart blisters cause constant pain if one does not take the time to properly care for and treat them. When we hike, we cover our blisters with Compeed, a great blister-blocking tape we found when we were hiking in Spain. (Of course, you can now find Compeed Advanced Blister Care Cushions on Amazon, like everything else.) The reason Compeed is better than a normal Band-Aid is that it holds on and won't let go. You need to find a friend who does the same thing, Mama. Treat your heart blister with friends and family who will hold on to you extra tightly. Don't despair; reach out.

And instead of incubating and insulating, try empathizing and encouraging. Taking an interest in others is the fastest way to forget yourself. When I feel heart blisters starting to form, I quickly find someone I can help. Sometimes that help looks like baking homemade bread for my elderly neighbor or watching my friend's young children. Often, helping takes the simple form of penning a note to a friend. What's the next right thing God has put in front of you? Figure out what it is, and then do it.

GRIEF IS REAL

Grief, in any form, is painful, and you never know when it will hit. It is entirely unpredictable. One day, you will be folding a shirt, and all of a sudden, a smell that reminds you of your loved one will flood through your senses and make you feel bittersweet. Or you will be cleaning out closets and find a once-loved Raggedy Ann with a stained mouth, and you will cry because it reminds you of your little girl. Or you will walk into the downstairs bedroom to locate the Republic of Chad on the previously mentioned wall-to-wall world map and instantly long for closeness with the son who once inhabited that room. In the delightful Christmas movie *A Boy Called Christmas*,[31] the main character says what we all know is true: "Grief is the price we pay for love, and worth it a million times over." Can I get an amen?

Though grief is a given, it doesn't have to end your hiking life. The trail goes on, and you can too. Remember my fat, salami-loving Neo? He died the summer after my Goer left and just weeks before our last child left for college. In the span of six months, our oldest son moved abroad, our youngest son departed for college, we became first-time empty nesters, and my beloved Neo passed away. I cry as I write this because, though it has been nearly seven years, the memories of that time still sting. I felt so helpless. Everything I loved was being stripped away from my life, and my sorrow was exhausting. I resonated with C. S. Lewis's observation about his own energy-zapping grief: "No one ever told me about the laziness of grief . . . I loathe the slightest effort."[32] Eventually, and with great effort, I swam through the molasses river of grief, but it took me much longer than I expected.

Still feeling a little blue? It's ok to feel sad. You won't hear me saying you can't cry (remember my tears on my son's birthday?). Let those tears flow, sweet sister. Just don't let yourself drown in them. Jordan Peterson, the author of the book *12 Rules for Life*, describes a "scheduled worrying" system that he used to control his anxiety when his young daughter was dealing with a painful and debilitating illness:

> Set aside some time to talk and to think about the illness or other crisis and how it should be managed every day. Do not talk or think about it otherwise. If you do not limit its effect, you will become exhausted, and everything will spiral into the ground. This is not helpful. Conserve your strength. When worries associated with the crisis arise at other times, remind yourself that you will think them through during the scheduled period. This usually works. The parts of your brain that generate anxiety are more interested in the fact that there is a plan than in the details of the plan.[33]

I employed a similar system to Peterson's to deal with the grief I experienced over my Goer's absence. During my morning routine, as I read the Bible and prayed for my family, I would record my thoughts regarding my Goer—both sorrows and joys—in a journal. As a creature of habit, I found this regularly recurring meeting with God and my prayer journal to be effective means of managing my worry. If I began to ruminate before a special event or during a sleepless night, then I would remind myself of my morning routine and attempt to lay the worry down. Most of the time, this worked for me.

Schedule your own grieving in a way that fits your life. Creating a plan will allow you to regulate emotions so your logical mind can contribute to the conversation. Navigating grief with your emotions on autopilot can make you feel powerless; navigating grief with a reasonable plan can provide a sense of control. By capturing our painful thoughts instead of letting them linger, we can remember the bigger story at work here: our children are offering Life to others.

When we take the time to process—not ignore—our grief, we invite the comfort and healing of God. And the comfort we have been given, we can share with others (2 Cor. 1:4). We sometimes walk through pain on this Missionary Mama journey, but we don't have to walk alone. God has promised to be with us, hot spots, blisters, and all.

Chapter 7
FALSE SUMMITS, SUFFERING, AND TRUE VIEWS

My family owns a ranch in northwest Wyoming that backs up to the Shoshone National Forest. Jim Mountain, with an elevation of 10,430 feet, is officially part of that forest, but it's right in our backyard! Needless to say, given our hiking history, we have ascended its peak many times. The climb takes focus and lots of determination, but the views at the top are truly breathtaking.

It wasn't always this way.

The first time I climbed it as a high-elevation newbie, I wasn't sure I would make it. The steepness literally stole my breath, and I had to stop every few steps to rest. Several hours into my first climb, I thought I saw the summit just over the next ridge. But when I reached it, I realized I still had farther to climb. After popping a Jolly Rancher in my mouth for quick energy, I kept trying to climb upward. I wanted to conquer this challenge, and fast.

FALSE SUMMITS

What I thought was the top is what mountain climbers call a *false summit*. A false summit *looks* like a real summit to the hiker because from his or her vantage point, the real peak is hidden. But as the hiker ascends to a higher plane, hoping and aching to be done with the climb, their perspective changes, and it becomes all too obvious that the top is actually very far away. False summits are disheartening to hikers.

Think through your Missionary Mama journey. Have you encountered false summits? I did, and they were just as deflating to me as when I encountered the real ones on Jim Mountain.

Several months after my Goer departed, I kept thinking maybe *this* book, or *that* hobby, or *those* new clothes would help me conquer my peculiar sorrow. But they didn't. They were poor substitutes—false summits—for true contentment. I was trying to suffocate my grief with things I thought would fill me with joy. They changed my view for a time, but as I continued my journey through these difficult times, I realized that they were not the true summit.

Ladies, God is our True Summit. He is the One we are trying to reach, the fulfillment of all our hopes. He promises that if we "seek first the kingdom of God and his righteousness ... all these things will be added to us as well" (Matt. 6:33). The "things" he speaks of include the peace, comfort, and rest that we crave. To "seek God first," we have to trust that he is good. And we have to trust him with our kids as well. False summits will lure you with the promise of ease, but they will leave you exhausted and sad.

Finding these false summits is kind of like suffering, but suffering can often result in something good. False summits hint at goodness, but in reality, they just wear us out.

SUFFERING

I'm not a huge television fan, but occasionally a Netflix series will grab my attention. The show *Alone* is one such series. Each season ten people are dropped in a remote location with a backpack that contains only ten survival items. The contestants' goal is to live off the land until they get incredibly lonely, seriously ill, or dangerously emaciated.[34] Though they have the option to "tap out" at any time, most contestants willingly endure great hardship for the chance to win a large sum of money. Because the participants can imagine how the prize money will enhance their lives, many of them voluntarily put their bodies and minds through extreme tests of endurance. When I think of fixing my eyes on God's promised eternal rescue, *Alone* comes to mind—as does the formula **a future reward > a present struggle**. Remembering this formula can help you avoid those enticing false summits and continue climbing towards the true views. It can also prepare you to view your *child's* suffering in a more positive light. Because, yes, they too will suffer.

Elisabeth Elliot reminds us, "If your faith rests in your idea of how God is supposed to answer your prayers . . . then that kind of faith is very shaky and is bound to be demolished when the storms of life hit. But if your faith rests on the character of him who is the eternal I AM, then that kind of faith is rugged and will endure."[35] We must look to Jesus, not our circumstances, if we want peace that endures.

While you are chewing on **a future reward > a present struggle**, add this little nugget to the menu: "but we also glory in our sufferings, because we know that suffering produces perseverance; perseverance, character; and character, hope. And hope does not put us to shame, because God's love has been poured out into our hearts through the Holy Spirit, who has been given to us" (Rom. 5:3–5). Suffering is not for naught; it achieves something good. Through our suffering we develop perseverance, character, and hope. These qualities make us more like Jesus. They make us better Mamas too.

TRUE VIEWS

I learned to climb to the top of Jim Mountain again and again by continuing past those false summits, but it's still a difficult climb. Even today, I sometimes suffer as I ascend the mountain. The same is true for me as I push through the Missionary Mama journey. I continue to work my way upward, though not without some struggle. But because I now see that **my future reward is greater than my present struggle**, my aches and pains seem worth it, and my heartache has begun to heal. Even though these heights are grueling, I am able to catch my breath and rest.

Up here in the clear air, my victories look different: their sole focus is no longer *me* or the removal of my discomfort, my grief, or my pain. I have gained a true view and a true victory by gazing on God's goodness and what he is accomplishing through my kids. They are living and loving and leading lost people. They are surviving and thriving and stretching. They are learning and growing and gaining new strength. They are looking a whole lot like Jesus. Really, what more could I want?

When we understand God's mission and meditate on his glory, it will make our problems seem lighter. As the apostle Paul says in 2 Corinthians 4:17–18, "For our light and momentary troubles are achieving for us an eternal glory that far outweighs them all. So we fix our eyes not on what is seen, but on what is unseen, since what is seen is temporary, but what is unseen is eternal."

Lately, as I have chosen to take the long view of eternity instead of the short view of affliction, I have found my heart beating with amazement rather than exhaustion and my mind filled with gratefulness instead of grief.

And now that my heartbeat is not so deafening, I can hear the glory of God's call to my kids.

I want you to hear it for your kids too.

So quiet your heart, open your ears, and fix your eyes on Jesus. He is your True View.

LAYERS OF LOVE

When I first saw you, I wondered who you were
And how you had gotten here;
So new,
So perfect,
So beautiful.

When I first heard you cry, I cried as well;
I knew you were mine.
And my love
For you
Was real.

When I first saw you in your daddy's arms,
I was struck by how much my heart could grow
With layers
Upon layers
Of love.

When I first held you on my lap,
Your small head cupped in my hands,
I marveled at how
I could cherish
Such a tiny stranger.

When I at last understood what undeserved grace
The Father above had bestowed,
I was overwhelmed
With gratefulness
And awe.

And now, because of you, I realize that I, too, am held
In my Father's arms, lavishly blessed
With layers
Upon layers
Of love.

After traveling abroad to meet my very first grandchild, I was struck by how my heart could expand to love not only my son (her daddy), but this perfect little girl as well. I wrote this poem as a love letter to her.

Chapter 8
"GRANDMA" IS MY TRAIL NAME

My husband, Brent, hiked a portion of the Appalachian Trail (AT) with our daughters when they were just nineteen and twenty-one. They had been hiking for six weeks before he joined up. Needless to say, they had gained their trail legs by this time and had the lungs to prove it. My husband tried his best to keep up with his adept and acclimated daughters but found it nearly impossible. After a few weeks, he adapted to their hefty mileage and quick pace, but not before he earned the trail name *Hot Water*.

A trail name is normally bestowed upon a hiker because of the mental image that forms when one sees them (e.g., *Gimli*), or because of a certain proclivity (e.g., *Preacher*), or, possibly, to showcase a laughable habit, like, let's say, heating precious water on a backpacking stove to bathe (e.g., *Hot Water*). Water on the AT was often scarce and had to be filtered or boiled to make it potable, so when my husband started to use some of this limited resource to wash his underarms and other areas, he earned the title *Hot Water*.

THE MOST PERFECT NAME

During this Missionary Mama adventure, I have (figuratively) gathered many names:

Mama Bear (I fiercely protect my cubs), *Waterfall* (I cry a lot), *Eeyore* (I can be a downer), and *Lollygag* (I travel at my own pace). But the name I love the very most, the most perfect of them all, is the name *Grandma*.

Grandma is my trail name, and it makes me a happy camper.

A JOYFUL ARRIVAL

When my overseas kids got pregnant and then delivered my very first grandchild, I was on cloud nine. Actually, I don't know the number of the cloud I was on because I flew through a bunch of them on my over-the-ocean flight to see her.

When our Goers called seven months earlier and told us we were going to be grandparents, Brent and I were thrilled! We immediately started planning our next visit. Though we didn't know if the baby was a boy or a girl, I started regularly perusing the baby section at Target while I dreamed of holding my new grandchild.

Then we got the call—two weeks before their scheduled due date.

Welcome, Baby Joelle! We had a granddaughter! Our Goers contacted us midmorning on a sunny day in April (even though it was late evening for them because of the thirteen-hour time difference) and told us the good news. They were exhausted;

they had traveled a full day, checked into a hospital, and delivered a baby, and now it was nearing midnight in their country. Meanwhile in Iowa, I was six miles into an eight-mile run, and I sprinted the last two miles home, struggling to breathe amidst my happy tears. I reached my husband, who was in the driveway looking for me as I finished up my run (they had called both of us on our cell phones) and who was equally stunned at the events that had just transpired. We had not expected Joelle to arrive so early, so we were planning to take a trip in early May and had not yet purchased tickets. Brent immediately got online to make the purchase as I gathered up the cute baby things hidden in the laundry room cupboard. We were on a plane to see our kids by 6 a.m. the next morning!

So many emotions crowded into my jet-lagged brain when, after twenty-six hours of traveling, we finally reached the hospital. I saw my son holding a tiny baby in a pink blanket. I said, out loud, "It's a real baby. It's *your* baby!" It was hard for me to comprehend that this new little human was a part of my son, which meant she was also part of me. THIS TINY HUMAN HAD MY DNA. I was blown away by her perfection, and my heart was full.

Until it wasn't.

A GRUELING GOODBYE

After spending six days with this new family of three in an Airbnb close to the hospital, our Goers left my husband and me early one smoggy morning. Since they had chosen to deliver the baby in a western-type facility in a nearby city, they needed to make their way back home via train. The minute the outer door clicked closed, I broke down in uncontrollable, breath-snatching sobs. I felt like a piece of my heart had been ripped from my body. I experienced an instantaneous feeling of loss. Even as I write this, nearly four years later, I am surprised at the tears that fall from my eyes. Separating from your kids is hard, but separating from your grandchildren—especially after just meeting them for the first time—is excruciating.

When your Goer has a child, you no longer just need a hiking buddy; you need a shoulder to cry on and someone to hold your hand. If you are a long-distance grandma, the time for hand-holding has begun right now.

That first goodbye was one of the hardest things I have ever done, because I knew I wouldn't touch my new granddaughter's face again for a very long time. Video-calls are wonderful gifts, but they can't transmit that intoxicating new-baby smell. So what did I do with my grief?

First, I collapsed into my husband's strong arms. Then after the tears and a walk to get some coffee, I mentally went back to the cairns to find my way. If you have forgotten the cairns, take a little stroll back to Chapter 5 and remind yourself.

REVISITING THE CAIRNS

When I looked for the Cairn of Gratefulness, I was able to thank my very generous Father for allowing me to become a grandma to a vigorous and healthy little girl. When I passed by the Cairn of Surrender, I told God how very hard it was to surrender the amazing gift I had just received—and that I didn't know if I could do it fully. I had to search for the Cairn of Freedom by focusing on what was good about this new situation.

Instead of indulging in self-pity, I thought about what was true: we would see our Goers and our precious granddaughter when they traveled back to the States for our youngest son's wedding in less than six months, and six months after that, we could schedule another trip to visit them overseas and see her in her own home. I visualized those visits as rewards for enduring this very real sacrifice. And besides those two visits, I could see her nearly every day on a screen if I wanted to.

Did I go through all these cairns consciously, intentionally passing them each in my brain? No. But because of the long, confusing "thru-hike" of my own Missionary Mama journey during which I had learned to follow these markers, my thoughts flowed fairly naturally; I had created healthy grooves of gratitude, surrender, and freedom in the pathways of my mind. You can do this too. Even if these thinking patterns don't yet feel natural, you can still consciously look for the cairns and learn to change your thinking.

Missionary Mama, maybe you have only recently become a far-away grandma and your heart longs to hold your new prize. Or maybe you have been on this grandparenting road for a long time and have worked hard for the trail name Grandma.

Either way, the first thing I want to say is that I'm so sorry. Most likely, *Virtual Grandma* is not the name you hoped for when you thought of this phase of your life. The second thing is that it can still be thrilling and fulfilling to influence your grandchild's young life, even when you are thousands of miles away. If you think of the distance as a challenge to be met rather than a roadblock to your relationship, then you can still have meaningful times with your kiddo. Believe it or not, they will get to know you through the screen and develop an affection for you. And you will be able to feel that affection when they visit the States and put their arms around you in a real, live hug. Virtual grandparenting is not exactly the same as having them close, but it still gives you an opportunity to spoil them a little and tell them how great you think they are.

CREATIVE CONNECTION

Want some creative ideas for connecting with your grandkids? Put some of these in your pack:

If your grandchild is just a baby, find an easy book that you can read to them every time you video call. Babies and toddlers find repetition comforting and will look forward to "Grandma's Story." When our granddaughter was obsessed with dogs, we read *The Puppy Book* dozens of times.

Ask your Goers to video call you when they are putting your grandchild to bed for a nap or for the night and sing them your favorite hymn or lullaby. Record yourself doing this and send it to them as an audio file so they can listen again and again. Our son loved when my husband sang "Living for Jesus"[36] to his daughter because he remembered his daddy singing it to him as a child. Remember to say a prayer of blessing over them before you are done.

Make a collage of family members' photos, attach it to an email, and have your Goer print it out. Then, the next time you video chat with your grandchild, go through the pictures and talk about all the relatives. Our granddaughter had a little photo album her great grandma created, and she loved to look at all the faces and say the names. When she was stateside, she could often recognize the people she had seen in the pictures, much to everyone's delight.

Employ a favorite toy. My husband's favorite way to communicate with our granddaughter was with props. He would find a doll or stuffed animal and proceed to make it talk in appropriate baby or animal language during our video chats with her. This thrilled our little one, who would continue to ask for him to "talk them," and it made her excited for our next call, especially if Papa was going to take part.

If you can easily send packages to your Goer, collect flat items like Kool-Aid packets, stickers, cute calendar pictures, sticks of gum, and photos of family members and send inexpensive care packages addressed to your grandchild. Send cards on real and invented holidays. And always, always sign them with lots of hearts.

If mailing is not an option because of unreliable delivery services, send videos back and forth using a video chatting app like Marco Polo. If the grandkids are a little older, host a cooking lesson where they follow along in their own kitchen.

Do your grandchildren like to play games? Then play one with them! Buy two sets of *Guess Who* or *Battleship* and send one with your Goer. Then, via video chat, challenge your grandkids to a friendly duel. (Tip: Let them beat you now and then so you can see them smile.)

Write to your grandchild in a journal on special days or just when you are missing them. When they are home, let them read these little love letters. Make sure to keep the journal, though, so you can continue to do this for them. What a treasure this will be to them if you continue to do it as they grow.

If your grandchild is a teenager, host a book club with them. Read a chapter each week and discuss it together on the weekends. This is a great way to share with them what you have learned and to have them do the same.

Memorize a Scripture verse together during your regular chats. You pick the verse one month, he/she picks it the next. Keep each other accountable and talk about why God's Word is important. Before my granddaughter was old enough to choose a verse herself, I taught her, "A glad heart makes a happy face" (Prov. 15:13 NLT), and sometimes, even if she couldn't remember the words, she would point to her rosy cheeks with her little fingers and smile (*happy face*) because that's how we said the verse. This made *my* heart very glad.

Pray for them specifically by name on one day of the month and ask God to give them a heart that truly loves him. I pray most days for my granddaughter, Joelle, but one day every month (each family member gets a regular day on my calendar), I pray an extended prayer for her and tell God how I long to play an influential role in her life.

If Grandma is your trail name on this Missionary Mama journey, remember this: even though you can't hold your sweet ones close right now, they have Someone near who can.

> "The beloved of the Lord rests in safety—
> the High God surrounds him all day long—
> the beloved rests between his shoulders."
> (Deuteronomy 33:12 NRSV)

God is surrounding our kids with his arms and lifting them to his shoulders. He is lifting you up as well.

Trust him. His trail name is *Father*.

PART 4
WHAT DO I DO NOW?

Chapter 9
LIVING OUTSIDE

Remember that trip to Alaska? Before we attempted to live outside in Denali, we were required to attend Bear Training at the ranger station. For those unfamiliar with this strange phenomenon, Bear Training teaches park visitors how to respond to a bear on the rare chance they are approached by one. After filling out paperwork absolving the national park of any responsibility should we be maimed or killed, we dutifully took our seats on yellow pleather couches and proceeded to watch videos about bears.

When the person in those videos was approached by an angry and teeth-baring grizzly, they steadily backed away, arms straight up in the air (to make them look as big as possible), calmly asserting "I'm a human!" over and over again until they were out of the attacker's visual field. After watching the assortment of dated but somewhat helpful videos, we were encouraged to partner up and practice the "I'm a human!" exercise until it felt natural. Luckily, we have an even number of people in our family, so each of us practiced this silly mantra with our closest of kin instead of with a stranger.

I'M A HUMAN

Thankfully, we never had to use our bear training on that trip, although it has provided much comic relief for our family ever since. And practically speaking, it has been helpful for me as a Missionary Mama:

» When I begin to chide myself for struggling so deeply with my child's absence in everyday life, I stop and remember "I'm a human!"

» When my siblings gather and discuss cute things their grandchildren did, and my grandbaby is so far away, it's okay for me to check out of the conversation because "I'm a human!"

» When I wish I could stop by and drop off cookies and just say, "Hi, y'all," I tell myself that is a normal mama desire, and I can go ahead and grieve because "I'm a human!"

» When I am preparing my holiday card and have a family picture with only part of the family, so I have to add a separate picture of my Goers in the corner, I can shed a tear of remorse because "I'm a human!"

» When all these pangs of sadness sneak in and I give my mind permission to see them as normal instead of silly, I am being authentic because "I'm a human!"

Being a human, and especially a human mama, means that I have emotions associated with my parenting role that will be sparked by certain circumstances or experiences.

Being a human means that I have joy, but also sadness; power, but also weakness; stability, but also fear. God designed us like this. In fact, "He knows our frame; he remembers that we are dust" (Psalm 103:14 ESV). We are not made of steel, nor marble, nor wood. We are made of flesh.

And sometimes that flesh is fine and fragile, like dust.

Sister, next time you are struggling with the fact that some of your favorite humans are not near, do the right thing: stand up tall, lift your arms in surrender, and say, "I'm a human!" A little grace goes a very long way.

BLOOM WHERE YOU ARE PLANTED

When I was a kid and would visit my aunt in the summer, I was always perplexed by a sign she had hanging over the sink in her kitchen. It said, "Bloom where you are planted." As a clueless ten-year-old, I assumed it had something to do with hippies. Growing up in the 70s had shaped my psyche, and I thought hippies and flowers were somehow associated with illegal drugs and free love. Because of that assumption, I kept my questions to myself and never inquired about the real meaning of the "bloom" sign.

Many years later, when I was studying the Old Testament book of Jeremiah,[37] I found this:

> This is what the Lord Almighty, the God of Israel, says to all those I carried into exile from Jerusalem to Babylon: "Build houses and settle down; plant gardens and eat what they produce. Marry and have sons and daughters; find wives for your sons and give your daughters in marriage, so that they too may have sons and daughters. Increase in number there; do not decrease. Also, seek the peace and prosperity of the city to which I have carried you into exile. Pray to the Lord for it, because if it prospers, you too will prosper."
> (Jeremiah 29:4–7)

What?! Build houses? Plant gardens? Seek the prosperity of this alien city? Do you know what God was saying to his chosen people through his prophet Jeremiah? In essence, he was saying, "Bloom where you are planted." I know this because as I got older and was less influenced by hippies, I figured out the meaning of my aunt's sign. It means, "Make the best of your situation."

LIVING IN EXILE

In the twenty-ninth chapter of Jeremiah, God was encouraging the Israelites, who had been captured by the Babylonians and forced to live in a foreign land, to stop resisting their new life. Basically, he told them to settle in for the long haul. And not only that, but he also wanted them to seek the peace and prosperity of this new city, because "if it prospers, you too will prosper."

If that was God's advice to people whose future looked different than what they had envisioned, then it's good advice for us too. Our future doesn't look exactly like we thought it would. We may feel like we are living outside our comfort zones. We may feel like we are living outside of the plan we have carefully crafted for our lives. But if we choose to invest in our present reality, in the days that God is giving us right now, our life will be "prosperous," and we will feel full, not empty. To be prosperous, we need to settle in and *choose* to thrive. We need to "bloom where we are planted."

My hero, Eugene Peterson, never minces words. Here is his take on this choice: "Exile (being in a place where we don't want to be) forces a decision: Will I focus my attention on what is wrong with the world and feel sorry for myself? Or will I focus my energies on how I can live at my best in this place I find myself? It is always easier to complain about problems than to engage in careers of virtue."[38]

How can you bloom when your emotional life feels so uprooted? First, go back and read about faulty and filtered thinking in Chapter 4. Then follow the Cairns of Gratitude, Surrender, and Freedom in Chapter 5. These practices will help you to adopt an attitude of abundance rather than lack, of celebration rather than complaining. Thomas Merton describes it well when he writes, "There are two kinds of people: some look at life and complain of what is not there; others look at life and rejoice in what is there."[39] Be the rejoicing kind of person. Then remember you are human and give yourself a break.

It might be time now to learn about some unexpected twists and turns you'll probably encounter on the trail. When we know about these twists and turns, we can stop blaming all our sorrow on our Goer's absence (or our own incompetence) and start figuring out what else might be weighing us down.

Chapter 10
A WOMAN IN THE WILD

In the wilderness, we sometimes encounter spur trails. A spur trail can be one of two things: a path that takes you off the main trail and leads to a beautiful view, or a trail that branches off and leads to a dead end. As I talk about spurs on our Missionary Mama journey, I am showing you the path *around* the dead end that leads to the beautiful view. I have been a wandering woman, but now I have found a good path. Walk with me.

Many Goers pursue their callings soon after they finish college (or at least in young adulthood) and within a few years of leaving home. Saying goodbye is always hard for mamas, but your tears may be caused by more than just your loneliness. This complicated season of sending often coincides with other major changes in a woman's life. If she doesn't heed the layers of stress that these added adjustments are causing, she might feel like a crazy woman wandering in the wild.

THE BIG THREE

»Menopause«

Let's start with the most taboo of the spurs: MENOPAUSE. Notice I put that in all caps because I am shouting it: MENOPAUSE, MENOPAUSE, MENOPAUSE! Maybe you are covering your ears now and looking around to make sure no one can see what you are reading. Maybe you are whispering, "Are we allowed to talk about that in a Christian book?" You bet we are, sister! Here we go!

Menopause messed with me. Even before it achieved its period-ending purpose (which is a great reward, by the way), it made me feel like a freak. Physically, I had few symptoms, but mentally, I felt like a hollow version of my former self. I didn't realize why I felt like this until a few years had passed and my hormones had leveled out. But with hindsight's better view, I can see how the spur of menopause led me down a dead-end path. No one told me that hormonal shifts could make me anxious and weepy for months at a time, but now, looking back, much of what I blamed on grief over my Goer's absence was probably amplified by menopause. Can you relate?

If so, here's my advice to you: if after some adjustment, you seem sadder than you should be as you send your child abroad, consider the changes going on in your body. Menopause can be a megaphone that makes the hot spots of this new life VERY LOUD. If you feel crazier than normal, meet up with your doctor and relay your feelings. There are many helpful natural (and not-so-natural) treatments to even out your moods. I didn't know my extreme insecurity was most likely a byproduct of menopause, but I could have enjoyed the view a lot more if I had asked for help sooner. Don't be embarrassed by your wobbliness, and definitely don't hike this spur by yourself.

»*Midlife*«

Brace yourself, Mama. Most likely, you are at the halfway point of your life (and that's being generous—do you really plan to live to a hundred?). When a woman is staring down the finish line rather than waiting for the gun to go off, her perspective changes.

Midlife has been somewhat of a conundrum for me. Physically, I feel great, and mentally, I have matured and become more emotionally sturdy. But I miss the life that once was mine, and memories of the past make this new season of maturity and freedom bittersweet. I loved the season of kids at home with all its busyness, family meals, and a sense of being needed. I loved developing little lives and felt like I was in my "sweet spot" as a stay-at-home mom. I loved the feeling, especially as the kids got older, of being a coach to help them shape their worldview. I loved that life when I was in it. I couldn't foresee the future being different. But let me tell you, it is.

So. very. different.

I have trouble with forward vision, so the empty nest came upon me just as I was gathering feathers of motherly insight and other useful items that would keep all my chicks cozy. Just when I got the sticks arranged exactly the way I wanted, all four of my birds flew away.

I was left with an empty nest and a hollow space in my heart. Hollow hearts in midlife often produce confused minds. Confused minds make us question our identity. My confusion about my new season made me feel like an awkward stranger in this new and quieter existence. I kept flitting around looking for myself in the now-empty rafters of my rationality, but I was gone, and someone else was living my life.

I'm sure this midlife meandering to nowhere—layered on top of menopause—made my Goer's absence seem all the more unbearable to me. Once I realized that I had put all my eggs of identity in the basket of motherhood, I was able to see the reverberations of this reality in my mental state and in my marriage.

»Marriage«

The third tier of additional stress during the time of my Goer's departure was produced by my view of my marriage. I now had a Dagwood sandwich[40] of adjustment to deal with: my son's absence combined with menopause and midlife and topped with marriage difficulties. All these ingredients piled atop one another made this period a time of deep sorrow for me.

Confusion about who you are can make you a bad marriage partner. Being a good partner requires us to deny ourselves often and choose to serve another. When I was in the throes of letting go of my full nest, my youth, and my identity, I longed to understand what was happening to me. Everything seemed extra hard, especially my relationship with my husband.

I was chronically unhappy and didn't know why. Processing my grief seemed to be taking soooo long, and I wanted to feel better about me. Actually, I wanted my husband to help me feel better about me, and I was mad because he didn't seem very helpful. He had greeted this new stage of freedom from family commitments with gladness; he chose to take trips and undertake projects in a way he couldn't do in the past. He seemed to be living his best life, while I was drowning in self-pity. I'm sure some of his newfound energy was a type of coping mechanism for him; he wasn't oblivious to the empty nest, the midlife reminders, and this crazy woman living beside him. But somehow, he seemed to take it all in stride. I assumed he wasn't struggling.

Now I know that he was confused by all the changes we were walking through together. He wasn't sure how to process all the unfamiliar feelings, so he chose to compartmentalize his grief in a way I couldn't. Because he is a thinker who tries to fit all of his musings into a logic-based grid in his mind, he was spending time quietly sorting while I was drowning in my tears. I resented him for his apparent balance and for his breezy approach to my complaints. During this time we fought. A lot.

I had to learn to look less to my now-grown children for love and belonging and more to my spouse for this emotional tank-filling. When I did this, our relationship began to re-blossom. This reacquainting with one another involved intentional effort and took the form of counseling with close friends, reading some marriage books together, and reinstituting a regular date night. We had spent the last twenty-six years of our marriage raising our family and being parents; now was the time to rediscover one another. The rediscovery has not been without some missteps, but we are on a much healthier path now and have an increased appreciation for the parts we each play in our shared life.

I tell you all of this *not* so you will feel sorry for my miserable plight at that time, but so you can feel the freedom to continue journeying through yours. Be aware of The Big Three as you send your loved one abroad. Don't pin all your problems on his or her absence. See all these variables as equal players. Just having an awareness of possible "dead-end spurs" in this Missionary Mama journey will help you to be a well-informed hiker, and a well-informed hiker is a more pleasant hiker, even if she wanders a bit (like me).

All who wander are not lost, though, because in my search for identity, I ran to God, and God led me to you. Missionary Mama, you have become my new passion; you are the renewed ministry that God intended for me all along. I hope that even as you read this, you can find yourself responding, "You too?"

> Maybe menopause has messed up your mind.
> Maybe midlife has been a surprise.
> Maybe your marriage is not full of joy.

I'm here with you, friend. Let us tame our wildness together.

Chapter 11
TRAIL MAGIC FOR YOU

Trail Magic, as defined by the Appalachian Trail Conservancy,[41] can include:

> » Finding what you need most when you least expect it;
> » Experiencing something rare, extraordinary, or inspiring in nature; or
> » Encountering unexpected acts of generosity that restore one's faith in humanity.

When my girls hiked the Appalachian Trail (the hike where *Hot Water* joined them in Chapter 8), they encountered a variety of trail magic: a local couple serving hot dogs and ice-cold root beer, a 4th of July fireworks show witnessed from a high mountain peak, and the occurrence of a perfectly timed miracle.

HEAVEN SENT SHOES

You could read that heading as *Heaven sent shoes* or *Heaven-sent shoes*. Either way is correct. My daughters experienced a sweet miracle from God when they needed it most.

My daughter Shay was hiking the northern half of the Appalachian Trail (AT) with her older sister, Tess. They were about 600 miles into an 1,100-mile trek (that is a true thru-hike, folks), and their shoes were starting to disintegrate. Many AT hikers choose to wear trail shoes rather than boots because they are lighter in weight and easier to get on and off. My girls had been wearing the same shoes up to this point in their journey and had each purchased and packed a new pair in a resupply box which I was to ship them from our home at the appropriate time.[42] Shay's shoes had begun to wear out a little faster than anticipated, and she had been mending them with duct tape and a needle and thread so they could remain functional until the box arrived in two weeks.

This particular day brought them into a town that boasted an "Outdoor Store," and Tess, being the older and slightly bossy sister that she is, told Shay she should stop and buy some shoes. Shay, being the younger and excessively frugal sister that *she* is, said she would just throw away the shoes there (they had become unusable) and hike the upcoming rocky terrain in her open-toed hiking sandals (yikes!). Why buy shoes when she would be receiving new ones soon?

This was not her best decision, and she regretted her choice.

Because they had fallen a bit behind schedule (they had to complete the trail by a certain date), after passing through that town, the girls decided to put in some serious miles to make up the distance. After hiking way into the night, they stopped at an AT shelter,[43] laid out their sleeping bags on the rough floor of the three-sided building, and went to sleep. Rising the next morning at the crack of dawn, Shay exited the shelter to visit the privy (most shelter sites have these little outhouses), and as she stepped out of the unwalled side of the cabin, she spied something sitting under the landing. Remember, when the girls arrived, it had been dark. Now, with the sun rising, Shay had a strange surprise awaiting her. As she went closer to investigate, she was flabbergasted when she saw a used pair of trail shoes—the exact same little-known brand as her now-discarded shoes, IN HER SIZE—sitting quietly under the shelter. Shay wears a women's size 12, ladies. This was a true miracle.

Not only was God watching out for my beloved daughters on that trip, but I'm sure he had a big smile on his face when Shay found her much-needed size-12 shoes. In the words of my very thankful daughter, "Not only were they the right size and in good shape, but they were also the same brand as my old shoes. God is good, and miracles still happen."

MAKING THE MAGIC HAPPEN

Missionary Mama, your shoes are probably fine as you continue on this long adventure, but your soul might need some mending. That's where Trail Magic comes in.

To review, one experiences the wonder of Trail Magic by:

»Finding what you need most when you least expect it;
»Experiencing something rare, extraordinary, or inspiring in nature; or
»Encountering unexpected acts of generosity that restore one's faith in humanity.

First, I want to show you how to discover Trail Magic for yourself, and in the next chapter, I want to encourage you to share it with others—specifically your Goers.

MAGIC FOR YOURSELF

When your kids are far away, you have to give up your expectations for the future. Kids grow up and begin to lead their own lives, and this is exactly what we want for them. Still, many of us look forward to sharing special times together, maybe even living close so we can see them often. Cheryl Savageau and Diane Stortz discuss this in their book: "There are cultural expectations for parents' relationships with adult children, and we can't entirely escape being molded by them. But we must learn to let them go."[44] Letting these expectations go is easier if you can visualize your child thriving in their overseas home. When you give up your desire to hold them (physically) close forever, you allow your Goer to live out their own hopes and dreams in a way you may not have envisioned. Exerting effort to support your child in their unique calling and culture will make them feel loved and will make you feel—magically—closer to them.

Here are a few tips that will help you **find what you need** (maybe when you least expect it):

As your Goer prepares to leave, or even if she's already gone, start to gather information about her new home—lots and lots of information. Educating yourself by researching your child's new city, culture, government, and language is a great antidote for anxiousness. According to Savageau and Stortz, "The more we learn, the more we are willing to understand, empathize, listen, and pray, the more we support our missionary and add action to our parental blessing. In turn, we are also blessed."[45]

In addition to gathering lots of information, ask your Goer

questions. Recently, I interviewed a new Goer who had been on the field for one hundred days. When I asked what he wanted the parents who were listening to know, he said, "Parents, we need more of you. Please ask us questions." Not only will you love your Goer by asking him questions about his life, but you will also become enlightened about your child's "far away existence" that seems so strange to you. What are some things to ask him?

> » How do you feel you are adjusting in your new culture?
> » Tell me the names of your team members. Who do you click with most?
> » Do you feel like God is teaching you new things as you do ministry?
> » How can I pray for you?

If you haven't already done it, give your blessing to your child. You can do this in a variety of ways. If they are already far away, speak it to them during a phone call or write an encouraging email. Tell them you are proud of them. Tell them that you support their decision to pursue missions abroad. Tell them how happy you are to be their mom. "Giving your blessing may be the most powerful thing you can do to allow your missionary to feel a close emotional connection with you despite the miles."[46]

The understanding you gain from educating yourself about your Goer's life doesn't just appear out of nowhere like actual Trail Magic; it takes commitment on your part. However, that commitment will pay you back with increased closeness and clarity. Confusion can be draining, but clarity has the ability to energize. And, sister, you need all the clarity and energy you can get for the journey ahead.

A second wonderful way that you might be blessed by Trail Magic is by **experiencing something rare, extraordinary, or inspiring** (in nature or otherwise).

Okay, so maybe it's not so rare anymore, but I still think it's extraordinary and inspiring that I can pick up the phone in my living room in Iowa, dial just a few numbers on my iPhone, and in moments a beautiful face will appear on my screen. Do you, like me, remember when the animated Jetsons family talked to their grandma on little TV screens, and how we all thought that was amazing and out of this world (and not just because the Jetsons lived in outer space)?[47] We live in that futuristic world right now, so put that jet pack on and make a video call. There are many, many ways to video chat with your Goer. I list several apps in the Appendix to get you started if you are technologically challenged.

Here are some specific ways we can keep in touch with our loved ones:

Establish a regular (but not suffocating) pattern of communication. For us, this is every other week. This may seem infrequent to some, but because of the time difference and the prolonged length of the video call, it works well for both families. Sometimes I felt guilty when other parents told me they talked to their kids daily, but we did what worked for us, and this was it. We will sometimes text or call during the intervening days, but we save the long stories for our scheduled video sessions.

Initiate a regular "family call" where siblings can join in on the call with you and your Goer. The practice of participating in a family video session has soothed my mama heart. Having all my kids in one place—even virtually—brings a sense of normalcy. Before our family call, each family member often sends photos to the others via our family text thread. This gives everyone a glimpse into the lives of the others.

Make a habit of sending your Goer little notes via text or email when you think of them. Don't just check in when something major occurs. When you see the Barbie School Teacher doll at Walmart, text your Barbie-loving daughter and tell her you would buy it for her if she were here. Allow yourself the freedom to send funny and completely unnecessary texts to your kids, because it will help them—and you—to feel like part of the family's normal life. This will also be good for your soul.

As you continue to search for surprises on the trail, look around your ordinary life for **unexpected acts of generosity**. Maybe they will restore your faith in humanity. Here are some that I have experienced:

Read about or take a course on missions. This may seem like a strange suggestion in the "generosity" Trail Magic section, but many churches offer these classes in person and online for FREE. They provide you with lots and lots of information—more than you could find on your own—and they fill your mind with knowledge you didn't know you needed. These classes may not have restored my faith in humanity, but I was awed by the faith of our Goers who are cooperating with God to restore humanity to himself.

One of my fellow Missionary Mama friends recently enrolled in an online course offered by her local church regarding missions. Contact your home church or peruse the website of your child's sending church to see if any such education is available to you. The IMB (International Mission Board) also has helpful resources and a variety of free online classes. You can check them out at imb.org.

Consider making the trip (more on this in Chapter 15, "Sky Hiking"). This is not only an incredible act of generosity towards your Goer (you are taking valuable time out of your own life to go and visit him in his), but it is also a real gift to yourself. If you can spare the expense and time (even if you need to get a prescription medication to help you with the very long flight), it will comfort you to be able to see (and later visualize) your kids in their own neighborhood; and they will be proud to show you their new home! Your visit will increase their confidence because the roles of parent and child will be inverted; they will be the guide, and you will be the follower. Being immersed in their everyday-ness will give you an appreciation for the lives they have chosen. A visit will also give you a chance to spoil them with a little TLC, along with treats found only in the States!

Trail Magic on this very long thru-hike can be just what you need to bring a little spring back to your step. Think of it as an extrapolated geocaching[48] session, and get started looking for the educational, relational, and informational treasures you will find.

Chapter 12
TRAIL MAGIC FOR THEM

I really, really wanted to send them a gift. It was probably more for me than for them, but the first Christmas that my kids were abroad, I packed a big box full of gifts. I wrapped each item in cute holiday paper, included some of their very favorite American treats, and carefully pasted their confusing address in both English and their Asian language (which I had to print from an email they sent because I had no idea how to write or type the characters) onto a mailing label. Then I lumbered off to the post office. Once I got there, I was required to fill out multiple customs forms where I had to list each item and its value in teeny tiny boxes. (One feels silly writing *Cheddar Blasted Goldfish Crackers* onto a government form, but I did so because I was a newbie and didn't know that level of specificity was not required.) Not only did this whole process take me the better part of an hour in a sauna-like post office, but the large box weighed nearly twenty pounds and cost me more than $200 to send. I was exhausted and alarmed and vowed that, even if my mama heart bid me so, I would never send another package abroad.

After six weeks of waiting, my Goers eventually got the package. They received some communication that it had arrived and, after days of searching, eventually tracked it down at a convenience store across town. They enjoyed their Christmas gifts—and their *Cheddar Blasted Goldfish*—in the middle of January.

Sometimes, especially during the holidays, the journey of being a Missionary Mama seems never-ending. Sometimes you just want to put your Mrs. Santa costume over your hiking clothes and deliver a little holiday Trail Magic to your Goer's house unexpectedly.

But when your kids live across the ocean, you won't be playing Mrs. Santa. You'll have to count on the real Santa to do his job, because he can fly all over the world in a sleigh—apparently in one night.

I don't know if you have attempted to send your kids a package or not. Maybe they are in a country with a more efficient mail system. Maybe the packages you send don't end up piled in a heap on the sidewalk outside the local noodle shop. Maybe it takes less than two months for them to receive mail from home. Regardless, here is what I have learned. America has a great system for mail and delivery, and I am very thankful for it—don't assume that the same system exists in countries abroad. Keep your head and heart happy by finding a non-postal way to provide Trail Magic for your kids. Here are a few ideas:

» Subscriptions: Subscriptions are a great gift that will last all year. You may be thinking "magazine subscription," and you could do this non-physically with ZINIO, but subscriptions to streaming services like Netflix or Audible (audiobooks) or gift cards for Kindle books, iTunes, or online courses might be more eagerly received. Ask your kids about delivery services that are available in their country; maybe you could send an actual physical gift through one of those as well.

» Annual Passes: Do your kids live in a large city with a zoo or an aquarium? How about a museum? Maybe a popular tourist attraction? A local pool? Possibly a rock-climbing gym? Research interesting venues that are close to your Goers, and then email them an online pass or gift card. If none of these possibilities exist, send them funds digitally (through Venmo, PayPal, etc.) and have them buy these gifts with the allocated funds.

» Experiences: Speaking of Venmo, it might be fun to send money specifically designated for a meal at a fancy restaurant, a manicure at a nearby spa, or even for a monthly purchase at the local flower shop. If you want to gift an experience to a married couple, consider tickets to a professional sporting event or concert. (Sometimes unfamiliarity with your Goer's culture makes this more difficult. A little online sleuthing or covert conversation with them could offer clues.) If you want to go really big, you could check different travel websites (such as Tinggly.com) and let your Goer choose their own experience!

» Support: Your Goer may also appreciate a one-time support gift from you or a donation to their sending church.

I realize non-physical gifts might not be as satisfying as watching your kids open actual gifts in your presence, but with a little creativity and some altered expectations, blessing them with a little Trail Magic can be rewarding for both you and your Goers. It can be fun for your kids to find an unexpected treat hiding on the trail. And they don't even have to put on their hiking boots to find it.

So, go ahead and indulge that Mama urge. You can't bless them with your physical presence, but you can spoil them with presents by sending some non-postal goodies. It's kind of like sharing some (virtual) *Cheddar Blasted Goldfish* together, except without the orange crumbs.

PART 5
WHEN WILL THE JOURNEY END?

Chapter 13
BEYOND GPS

In the first week of August 2017, my husband and our youngest son, Cole, flew to Tanzania to climb Mount Kilimanjaro, the highest mountain in Africa. They were part of a group called *Mountain Professionals* who lead guided climbing expeditions to summit the world's highest peaks. Our Goer and his sister, who was staying in his host country that summer for a short-term mission trip, also flew into Tanzania and met up with their father and brother to join them on this once-in-a-lifetime experience. Our other daughter had started her first job and wasn't able to join them. And I'm only moderately adventurous and only kind of brave (this trip required a level of courage I *do not* possess), so I stayed home and ate tortilla chips and watched Downton Abbey with my dog.

CUMULATIVE GROSSNESS

Forty-eight hours after arriving, the group of thirty-two (twelve hikers plus twenty sherpas and support staff) started their trek up the iconic mountain. The summit would take five days.

Days one, two, and three were pretty typical hiking days, but on day four, the group camped at the Kilimanjaro high camp. *High camp* is the highest elevation campsite (this one is 16,732 feet) at the base of a mountain and above the tree line,[49] where climbers stay the night before they intend to summit. Because they needed to reach the top before the typically unpredictable afternoon weather arrived, the group disappeared in their tents by 7 p.m. so they could rise in the middle of the night and get trekking by 1 a.m. on day five.

Cole struggled to sleep that night at high camp. The air was very thin, and his heart rate measured 110 beats per minute even as he attempted to rest. All too soon he climbed out of his sleeping bag into the frigid air and prepared to hike up the mountain. Because it was only 1 a.m., and because he had barely slept, Cole was groggy when the group, all of whom were wearing headlamps so they could see their trail, set out. As he hiked, and as the hours passed, he began to get worse and worse (*cumulative grossness* were his words) until he felt dizzy, drunk, confused, and completely exhausted. His brain kept shouting at him to lay down and go to sleep, but on the craggy mountainside, sleeping wasn't an option. It was difficult for him to think logically when his brain kept telling him that moving was impossible, even though his body was physically sound.

FOLLOW THE LEADER

The group stopped to take a break just as the sun appeared. Ryan, the watchful guide, noticed Cole looking strange and approached him with a pulse oximeter to measure the oxygen in his blood. After taking the reading (which Cole later learned was 72/100!), Ryan immediately left and brought back hot tea and some altitude sickness medication. He gave them to Cole, who at this point was fighting to stay conscious. Then Ryan gave him some very specific instructions: "When you start walking, follow the footsteps of the person in front of you."

Emboldened by the hot tea, medicine, and beautiful sunrise, Cole was eventually able to shake off his sluggishness. Finally, a few hours later, after stepping in each footstep of the person in front of him, Cole made it to the top alive along with the rest of the group.

When a person hikes at high elevation, the oxygen gets thinner, and the body can't easily process it. The five-day hike up Kilimanjaro was designed to acclimate the hikers so that the adjustment to higher altitude would be easier. Cole's muscles and ligaments seemed to be okay with the change, but his mind and feelings—the GPS system of the body—were going haywire in response to the lack of air.

Just as the Global Positioning Systems that we use on our phones can help us to navigate in unfamiliar places, God designed the GPS of our brains—our feelings and intuition—to help us gain homeostasis when we are feeling a little off balance. But when that natural GPS system fails to perform, either because of physical trauma (like what unacclimated Cole experienced trying to climb Mount Kilimanjaro), or because of emotional grief (like we face on the Missionary Mama journey), we may need to find another way to hike.

Maybe your journey has made the air seem thin. Maybe your GPS is telling you to stop. If that's you, I am here to say, *As you move forward in this journey, follow the footsteps of the person in front of you.*

That's me. And that's all the other parents who are doing what you're doing right now.

I've interviewed them on the Parents of Goers Podcast.[50] I've talked to them on the phone. We've enjoyed coffee in the church foyer after their kids were commissioned to go abroad.

This climb has been hard for them too.

But we have walked this road before you, with its seemingly undefined endpoint, and we can promise that if you keep going, if you keep following us step by step, you will soon start noticing the sunrises, the amazing view, and the "hot tea" of Missionary Mama friendships, which are good medicine for your soul. When you learn to go beyond the false summits of your expectations, you can take in the true view, even if it seems like you're hiking very slowly and for a very long time.

ADJUSTING YOUR PACK

Friend, if you have gotten this far in the book, you've learned about *God's mission*, about your *child's vocation*, and about *faulty* and *filtered thinking*. You know how to locate the Cairns of *Gratitude, Surrender, and Freedom* when the *hot spots and blisters* flare. You can identify *false summits*, understand why you are *suffering*, and look for the *true views*. You can enjoy your *virtual Grandma* role while you *bloom where you are planted* on this journey through the *wilderness*. You are aware of *The Big Three* and can factor them into the equation of your loss. You know where to find the *Trail Magic* for yourself and your Goer.

Now it's time to adjust your pack and reorganize your expectations for the future.

Hikers often have to remove their backpacks if they are causing hot spots or are feeling too heavy. Maybe they are carrying too much weight and need to hand some off. You might be feeling this way right now on your Missionary Mama journey.

As you are following in my footsteps, you may say, "Hey wait, this pack feels too heavy." That's probably a sign that you need to adjust your expectations for the future. Let me help you carry some of the heavy stuff.

When my son was stateside for a few months after he had been on the field for a couple of years, he went to visit his old high school track coach, who asked him, "When are you going to get this out of your system and find a real job?" This misconception about the "realness" of our Goers' jobs was not encouraging to my son. He *was* doing a real job, and he was obeying God's call on his life. It hurt him that his beloved coach didn't respect the life he had chosen.

If you, as a Stayer, have a bit of that attitude swimming around in your brain, you probably need to adjust your pack. Decide to stick with this journey for the long haul. When we, as parents, express our dissatisfaction with our children's absence by asking again and again when they are coming home, it is discouraging to them. Maybe they have agreed to a specified time of service; more likely, however, they are just taking things day by day and don't know what the future holds. They may plan to stay in their host country long-term. As a mom, I know it's hard to plan your future when you don't know what it holds (though we never *really* know anyway). Like the hikers on the early-morning Kilimanjaro hike, we only have a headlamp to light our way. A headlamp provides us with just enough light to take the next step. So, keep walking, mama, even if your feet feel heavy and your brain is telling you to stop.

CHOOSING WISE WORDS

If the Covid-19 pandemic taught us anything, it was that we are clearly NOT in control. Because we couldn't control this intrepid invader, we clung to the things we *could* control by wearing masks, washing our hands, and trying to limit our exposure to the virus. We took these small (and wise) steps because doing so gave us a feeling of security when it seemed like things were out of our control.

I used to think that if I could control all the variables in my life—my son's future return included—then I could rest comfortably and avoid feeling fear. But, in reality, I can never do this. I have only a headlamp's worth of insight, just like everyone else. My finite mind will never be able to give me all the answers or show me what's next. But by placing my faith in an infinite God who *does* know and who wants what's best for me, I can peacefully proceed on the path.

Speaking wise words when the future is unclear requires determined self-awareness. Be careful how you talk to your Goer about things. Remember you are to be her cheerleader and not her critic. Use wisdom when you talk about the future and about her plan to return "home." One of the most effective ways we can bless our kids is by encouraging them right where they are. Obvious parental dissatisfaction weighs heavily on our kids. Cheryl Savageau, co-author of *Parents of Missionaries,* observes:

> Large numbers of potential mission recruits never make it to the mission field because they do not re-

ceive a parental blessing. Some missionaries return prematurely from the field because of strained family relationships. Parents, missionaries, and sending organizations need to recognize the value of healthy parent/adult-child relationships and take active steps to help parents of missionaries and their missionary children maintain strong bonds across the miles.[51]

A careful adjustment of the pack you are carrying will often help you prolong your child's time of service, *and* it will be a great encouragement to him. How do you make these adjustments? You need to reorient your mind to accept an indefinite endpoint, and you need to hand off the things that are too heavy by sharing your anxiety and concerns with others, especially other Missionary Mamas.

Hang in there, hiking buddy, and choose to embrace the uncertain nature of your Goer's future. Uncertainty causes us to feel our need for God more acutely. And as the Bible teacher Nancy DeMoss Wolgemuth often tells us, "Anything that makes us need God is a blessing."[52]

Chapter 14
SHARING THE CAMPSITE

When our family hiked together on popular hiking trails, we were always slightly disappointed if we arrived at the campsite where we had planned to stay the night and someone was already there. If the site offered more than one spot for setting up tents, we would unburden ourselves, pull out our tents, and choose to live harmoniously with our new hiking friends. If the site was too small to share, we would have to continue our hike, maybe for several miles, until we came upon another, less-populated site. Having our own space was often worth the extra distance because we could yell from tent to tent, laugh uproariously at inappropriate jokes, and eat our supper without others spying our delicious chili-mac. The freedom to do our own thing made us happy. But sometimes, when we were tired and worn from walking, the extra miles—and the other people—just made us mad.

Furlough, the glorious idea that has danced in your head from the moment your Goer departed, might make you feel like you are sharing a campsite if your kids live with you during the time that they are home. And you may find yourself feeling like your campsite is crowded, especially if you've become accustomed to a tidy tent, easy meals, and quiet evenings by the fire.

THE COVID CONUNDRUM

"We're coming home!" They were the words I most wanted to hear during a time I most wanted to hear them: the Covid-19 pandemic. This daily tension of watching the news and waiting on information from our Goers was unexpectedly broken with a cryptic-sounding pre-dawn phone call in early February: "We got out twelve hours before the country closed its borders. We fly out in the morning." I hung up the phone, sat in the darkness, and cried.

God was still in control.

After a safe flight home and two weeks in self-imposed quarantine, our kids and their team members each joined their families for an unexpected furlough. I was both thrilled and saddened by this turn of events; thrilled because I would have my loved ones close (living in our basement!), and saddened because I knew they had to leave their own homes and friends and ministries behind. The future looked uncertain for both of us.

THE FURLOUGH FALLACY

As Covid wore on, I secretly loved the fact that my kids' return date to their host country kept getting pushed further and further back; it meant that they would be in the States for family times at the lake house, their birthdays, and maybe even Christmas. I knew it made them uncomfortable to have no clear plan for the future, but their unforeseen arrival had soothed my aching heart. Knowing that they had just endured upheaval, fear, and uncertainty, I was anxious to mother them and make them feel safe. In my exuberance, I made some assumptions about their furlough that added stress, rather than joy, to their unexpected presence in our lives.

CAMPSITE CRASHERS

The only experience I have with extended furlough thus far in my Missionary Mama journey is the result of Covid. Coronavirus reared its ugly head in late December 2019 in Wuhan, China, and it soon made its destructive way around the world.

When humanity gets hit with a worldwide pandemic, everyone's plans get upended. Many missionaries, who were understandably anxious about the uncertainty of this unfamiliar virus, left their host countries and headed back to their passport countries, thinking they would only be gone for a short time. Some chose to go; some were forced to go by their organizations. For some workers, their time away was a matter of months; for others, it dragged on for more than a year (maybe two); and for some, it ended their time abroad.[53] Many Goers who had to leave their host countries still express deep sadness about this unforeseen turn of events. At the time of my Goers' arrival at our home, it was impossible to know what the future would hold.

Prior to the Covid development, I had a vision of what my Goer's future furlough might be like for me. When I found out they were leaving their overseas home and traveling back to the States, I was relieved—and excited—that I could offer them some protection from this scary disruption. But when they got here, the much-anticipated time together felt very different. In a way, I think both families (Stayers and Goers) felt like the other had "invaded their campsite."

My feelings of joy mixed with irritation confused me and ushered in guilt. How could I be unhappy when my precious ones were close enough to touch?

I learned so many lessons about myself during this unexpected Covid campout. I saw that my desire for control made me grumpy, that unforeseen transitions made me anxious, and that I thought I could read the minds of everyone around me (it turns out I can't). Mostly, as I have preached in previous chapters of this book, I learned that a little grace goes a long way.

And a lot of grace makes me more like Jesus.

THE FURLOUGH REALITY

Since our kids were now home, I assumed they would be *happy* to be here, *grateful* for my motherly care, and *eager* to spend time doing normal "family things" together. In reality, though, here is what happened:

They weren't happy about their unexpected furlough. Of course, they were glad to see us and loved the soft beds and the easy access to a washing machine, but life as they knew it had ended for a time. Their abrupt retreat from the country they had called home for four years made them feel guilty and grieved. They wondered why God would put a passion in their hearts to minister across the ocean and then whisk away their life of service with the onset of a global pandemic. They were confused and saddened by their sudden change in circumstances.

They struggled to be grateful as they adjusted to their "new-old" American culture and family expectations. When the kids showed up on my doorstep, I was eager to serve them. I shopped and cooked and cleaned and watched our granddaughter whenever I was asked. It was the least I could do for them, I figured. But as days wore on and I continued to do the lion's share of these tasks, I became resentful of what I perceived as their lack of gratitude. In my well-worn motherly way, I overfunctioned. I wanted to do it all and told them so (even though they had offered to help), but I was now tired and wished that I had established clearer expectations for both families. As I spent more time with them, I also realized that they were experiencing reverse culture shock; they were trying hard to be thankful while resisting the urge to judge their families who were living—even if moderately—in this excessive American culture.

They needed to spend time alone to process what had just transpired. When our kids arrived home, I had visions of spending time over coffee with them each morning and having long, meaningful discussions in the evenings. We had so much time to reclaim. I assumed that since they were no longer "working," they would want to hang out with us, right? Wrong. My son had quickly left his country, flown on several airplanes, quarantined with fifteen other people, and been plopped down in his childhood home as a nearly twenty-nine-year-old man. As a team leader, he felt the weight of making wise decisions for both his peers and his family. He had leadership responsibilities in his church abroad. He had to think prudently about the future of his ministry. Sometimes, I'm sure, he was second-guessing his calling. He and his wife and daughter had, in essence, endured trauma in this unwelcome pandemic. They needed to pray and process and lament apart from us. They had plenty of work to do but felt enormous pressure to spend time with family and friends. The unstated assumption of increased family bonding only made their internal angst all the more difficult to process.

THE GIFT OF GRACE

Once I realized that I had errant expectations about how this furlough time would transpire, I chose to do some of my own lamenting. It wasn't wrong for me as a parent to expect to have joy when my child returned; I had missed him so much. My error was in thinking that having him home would make me feel fulfilled. My faulty reasoning showed itself in sadness and resentment when he wasn't *happy, grateful,* or *eager* to spend time with us.

My satisfaction with my life will always be lacking if I rely on my circumstances or on other people to give me joy. My contentment comes not from being in complete control of my future, but from choosing to trust that God has allowed things to happen in my life to make me more like him. In an unexpected furlough, as in all things, true satisfaction comes through Jesus and his finished work on the cross—for me, my kids, and all those who call on his name, both here and across the ocean.

Without a doubt, God was still accomplishing his purposes during this unexpected furlough, and I needed to reorient my thinking and change my perspective so I could be an agent of grace for however long we were all under one roof. I was offered grace when my eternal future was uncertain; why should I not repeat the favor in a small way to my kids? Here is a GRACE acrostic I created at that time so I could change my faulty thoughts about my furlough "hardship" by filtering my thoughts with truth. Maybe this filtering can help you too:

Give them the benefit of the doubt. If they seem ungrateful or inattentive, assume they are processing their past experiences or wondering about the future. Going back to their home culture—and especially living with parents—can require some major adjustment.

Readjust your expectations to fit your desires and abilities. Do you want them to assist with household tasks or meal preparation? If so, let them know the ways they can help. Making roles clear will help them know how to contribute and allow you to do your work with more joy.

Ask them how they are feeling about their lives. What makes them happy? What makes them sad? What are their hopes for the future?

Create a serene environment for them. Slow down your life for a time so you can focus on these very precious ones who are physically present with you. You will be so glad you did this when they finally say goodbye.

Enjoy! They won't live with you forever. Intentionally build relationships with your kids and grandkids while they are living under your roof. Make memories that will sustain you when they are far away.

Missionary Mama, maybe your child won't return for an unexpected time of furlough because of a global pandemic. Maybe sharing a campsite is easier for your family than it was for ours. Even so, your Goer's furlough may look and feel differently than you expected. Remember that you are the only one who can determine your attitude about this time. If you choose to be grateful for the wonderful privilege of having your kids close by, then your responses to yourself and your loved ones will make you—and all those sharing your site—courteous and cordial campmates.

Chapter 15
SKY HIKING

As our children got older and their experience in backpacking grew, we allowed them to plan some of our hiking trips. Over time we learned that this was a bad idea, since one's prefrontal cortex, the brain's rational part, is not fully developed until age twenty-five.

On one of these particular trips (organized by our then twenty-year-old daughter), we decided to spend our Christmas break in the sunny south. We rented an RV, packed up all our gear, and took a couple days traveling from Iowa to supposedly warm (but actually very chilly) Arizona. Our goal was to complete a hiking loop near the Superstition Mountains.

As we neared our destination, we realized that the Apache Trail listed on our daughter-created itinerary was the only road that would take us to our starting point. If the Apache Trail had been a normal mountain road, this wouldn't have been a problem. However, this route was an ancient foot path once used by the Apache Indians, and apparently it had not improved since that time. This trail was a forty-mile, narrow, single-lane, mostly unpaved path with steep drop offs, and there was a sign at the beginning of the route that discouraged taking large trucks or RVs on the unmaintained road.[54]

My husband, who was driving at the time, decided that he was up for the challenge. I was not pleased. Fearing for my life and the lives of my children, I made my way back to the queen bed in the rear of the camper where I proceeded to cry while my fifteen-year-old son held my hand and quoted Psalm 91. When we miraculously arrived in safety at our chosen trailhead, I said, "I am NOT going to do that again! You are going to have to shoot me to get me out of here!" Long story short: we went out the very same way we came in. They didn't shoot me.

Sometimes flying—what I like to call "sky hiking"—is a better option than rumbling along on the mountain roads. And sometimes, as in the case of visiting your Goer, it's the only option. Our kids live far away, and sometimes the trip can seem overwhelming, even if your brain is fully developed. For many Stayers, sky hiking across the ocean in a jetliner seems nearly as impossible as driving on an ancient footpath in a massive RV.

I CAN'T DO THAT!

As part of the requirements of adulting, you may have to do things you think you *can't* do. Flying on several long flights to the other side of the world is something most people don't do very often, so it may be hard for you to wrap your head around the whole process, and you may find yourself fearing the unknown. Perhaps you have never gone on a long flight. Maybe you've not flown at all. This was the case with my friend Diane. When I interviewed her about her decision to visit her Goer in

China, she told me that before she made the trip, she had never flown on an airplane. That's one way to jump right in! When I asked her if she had ever expected to visit, she told me, "My heart said yes. My anxiety said no."[55]

TELLING YOUR ANXIETY "YES"

How do we help our heart win out over our anxiety?

This is how Diane did it: "We started making plans. Then it started getting real. We were buying tickets and suitcases, getting ready for the trip. I busied myself with a thousand packing tasks to just keep moving forward. Finally, I just broke down and said, 'God, I am praying boldly for you to take this fear that I'm handing to you and get me on that plane. My daughter needs her parents.'"

In faith she persevered.

They chose to break the trip into chunks. The first trip was a short flight to a city about five hours from their home. They figured if the whole flying thing didn't work out, they could drive home from there. As they were driving to the airport, walking to the gate, making their way down the long ramp to the first flight, Diane kept telling herself, "Keep going. Keep going." But when she stepped on the plane and saw three seats on one side and two on the other, she immediately felt claustrophobic and said to herself, "Nope. I'm not going to do this." In desperation she turned to her husband, Andy, who was wearing the biggest "Dad smile" on his face as he exclaimed, "We are going to see our daughter in twenty-four hours!" Emboldened by her husband's joy-filled reminder and driven by her love for her Goer, she acted in faith and put her seatbelt on. Sitting in her seat, almost as if God himself was nudging her, she remembered a sermon she heard at their church recently where the pastor reminded them, "There are times in your life when you just want to be able to say at the end of it, *God did that.*"

They survived that first leg. The next flight was to the west coast, where they spent the night and got some rest, some food, and a shower before the fourteen-hour flight to Shanghai. They figured they could also drive home from Seattle if need be. When they got to the coast, thanks to their practice flights, they felt like flying wasn't that big of a concern anymore. "My husband and I were just having fun doing something different and new together." Now refreshed from their night at the hotel, they boarded the plane the next day and flew across the ocean to their daughter.

I CAN DO THIS!

Diane was able to fly across the ocean because she believed God was bigger than her fears, and she believed he would do what was best for her. In this case, his best was a beautiful and uneventful fourteen-hour flight across the ocean (and back) with "ice cream and as many desserts as you wanted." Because she was not anxiety-free, and because she expressed her fear openly, she could never take credit for successfully undertaking this seemingly overwhelming journey. Obviously, *God did that* and allowed her to make the trip.

Maybe you can't do it. Diane couldn't. But God could—and did. Do you need to surrender your anxiety to God so you can visit your Goer? Here are some practical steps to move you in that direction:

Rather than letting your panic spiral, speak about your fears out loud to someone to disarm them. Diane spoke directly to the stewardess who was managing her section. She said, "I've never been on a plane before. Could you check on me once in a while?" The stewardess happily complied and brought her snacks, hot towels, and encouragement. Diane felt cared for because she was proactive in disarming her fear rather than letting her fear take control.

Talk to people who have made a similar trip. What was hard? What was easy? Is there anything I need to do to prepare?

Make sure you have a valid passport. If your passport is set to expire within six months of your travel date, the authorities in the country you're traveling to may not accept it. Make sure you're aware of visa requirements too, as they are specific to each country.

Visit the U.S. Post Office online at www.usps.com and request a mail hold, or have a neighbor pick up your mail and packages while you are gone. It's a dead giveaway that no one is home if mail is ignored and packages are piled by your door.

Speaking of being obvious, hold the social media posts about being across the ocean until you are home again. Nothing says "burglary target" more than advertising your extended absence from your house.

Think about your reward. I quote Diane again: "It was a very long trip of ups and downs and sitting in airports—thirty-two hours of traveling in all—but when I got to the airport in my Goer's city and saw my daughter jumping up and down in joy, it was totally worth all the anxiety we felt, the money we spent, and the energy we expended to get there."

Medication can be a huge help. It allows your mind to relax and your body to cooperate. Don't be ashamed if you need a prescription of anti-anxiety pills to allow you to see your child. Call your doctor, tell her what's up, and she will gladly help you out.

I'M DOING IT! I'M DOING IT!

When my Goer first learned to ride a two-wheel bicycle, he soared by me as I sat smiling on the front step, and he yelled, "I'm doing it! I'm doing it!" He wasn't sure he was up to the challenge, but he decided to be brave and succeeded.

One year after successfully completing the trip to China, Diane and Andy decided to go again! The first trip had given them confidence, so they knew they could rise to the challenge of making a second one (this time to see a newborn grandbaby!). Because of their familiarity with the exhausting process of going abroad, they felt more prepared and less uneasy the second time around. I also felt this way when we went abroad our second, third, and fourth times. When you know the path ahead of you, it seems easier to follow.

Sky hiking can be an enjoyable experience if you heed some simple instructions:

Although airports and flight tracking are inherently confusing, downloading an app like GateGuru to help you find your way around an unfamiliar airport or FlightAware to track your incoming or outgoing flight will help. Many airlines also offer their own apps that will alert you to changes in your itinerary.

I like to have a printed copy of my ticket even if I have an electronic version because sometimes my phone won't cooperate with me or the airport associates.

When my husband and I go abroad, we pack very lightly (we are backpackers after all), only taking carry-on luggage that can fit above our seats on the plane. Not only does this help alleviate worries about lost bags, but it also saves us time when passing through International Customs.

Speaking of Customs, this term "refers to the agency that international passengers need to go through when attempting to cross international borders and bringing goods into the country that may be restricted, such as food or substances prohibited by law."[56] The Customs agents must ensure that travelers comply with the rules and regulations of the new country. When you arrive at your destination country, you will need to fill out a Customs form where you state the purpose of your trip and declare any items you will be bringing to your country. Have your passport ready to present to the officer. Getting through Customs can take a long time if you arrive at the same time as thousands of other people. Just be patient and smile at all the babies (and be glad you are not traveling with one).

Speaking of speaking, it's super helpful to at least expose yourself to the language of your child's new home. I did this by using a Rosetta Stone program on my computer, but it is just as helpful to learn some simple phrases like "I am hungry" or "I am lost" by purchasing a phrase book in the language you want to learn. Google Translate is also incredibly helpful for communicating with local people.

Flying in economy class (the only way I have ever flown commercially) is never super comfy. Occasionally, we have been able to score *Premium Economy* or *Economy Plus* seats, which are a little larger and wider. This is especially wonderful since my husband is 6'6" and I am close to 6'. Here are a few simple tips to increase your comfort wherever you end up sitting:

For flights that are longer than a couple of hours, it's wise to wear compression socks. Since the opportunities to stand, walk, and stretch are limited on these long flights, blood can pool in your legs. Wearing compression socks can help promote circulation and prevent swelling in your lower legs and feet. If you are worried about looking elderly in your stockings, don't buy them at your local pharmacy—search "fun compression socks" on Amazon and sport some snazzy ones instead.

Make sure you drink plenty of water when you are flying. If you are like me and detest the tiny bathrooms, this may be hard. Do it anyway, because airline cabins are pressurized, which means less fresh oxygen is getting into your system. Getting less oxygen can cause dehydration, and dehydration can make jet lag worse (and generally make you feel bad).

Here's a well-known international traveling mantra: West is best; east is a beast. What does that mean? It means jet lag tends to be worse when traveling from west to east. Why? Dr. Kieran Seyan explains it like this: "In short, your body's natural rhythm follows a 24.5-hour day, slightly longer than the standard 24-hour sun-up, sun-down rhythm. That means that if you're traveling east over many time zones, you'll 'lose' additional time. In a way, you're traveling forwards in terms of hours and days, arriving ahead of yourself, which requires your body to be 'advanced.'"[57] While you can't avoid jet lag, you can still try to train yourself to adjust faster by sleeping on the plane when it is nighttime in your destination, even if it's the middle of the day at your home. When you get to your child's country in the daytime, aim to stay awake until you absolutely can't make it anymore. I once went to bed at 6:30 p.m. on the first day we visited because I could no longer function. Getting some exercise and some sunshine during your initial days in country can also help to reset those circadian rhythms.

Your American dollars likely won't be very helpful in a foreign country. Make sure you exchange currency before you leave or after you arrive. There are a variety of ways to do this, but be wary of the airport exchange kiosks as they often charge large fees and give a much lower exchange rate. They have a captive (and often clueless) audience, and they take full advantage of that fact.

One of the best ways to get foreign currency is by exchanging money at your local bank or credit union before your trip.

If your local bank does not have the foreign currency, they can often order it, or you can procure it from a currency conversion website like OFX.

There are always fees to change your money no matter how you do it, but you can avoid some of them by withdrawing cash from an ATM in your destination country. This is an especially smart move if you have a bank with low or no foreign-transaction fees.

If you plan to use your credit card in a foreign country (many countries accept the major ones) or even in the airports, contact your credit card company so they won't be surprised by purchases accrued on the other side of the world and you won't be surprised by them freezing your account.

I'M SO GLAD I DID!

When Diane made the trip to see her Goer, she gained admiration and appreciation for what her daughter was doing and for who she had become. Not only had her daughter learned a difficult foreign language, but she could now easily navigate a large city via public transportation as well. I was likewise awed at my Goer's adeptness with the language and his ability to communicate with locals while I was there. Visiting your child abroad will give you a sense of the tremendous effort it took for your Goer to adjust to this fascinating new culture that they now call home.

On top of the reward of spending time face to face with your Goer, their newfound confidence and pride in their new home will allow you to view them differently. When you visit, the typical roles of leader (parent) and follower (child) are somewhat flipped. Because your child has lived in this new place for a time, he is now the expert, and you are the newbie. It can be appropriately humbling to have to rely on your child to successfully survive during your visit. It is fun to see them in this role, so let them lead.

Let them lead you to their vegetable lady and to the place they go to school. It will help you visualize them in these places when you return home. Let them assist you at the grocery store so you don't buy what you think is cinnamon-raisin bread and have it turn out to be red bean-paste bread instead. Ask them to help you understand the different customs and social mores so that you aren't offensive to the locals. Do life with them as they are living it, even if that means you have to adjust to using a squatty potty or dining with unfamiliar eating utensils. Speaking of eating, don't be afraid of trying some delicious new foods. Eating local cuisine is another way to connect with your kids' experiences.

Be careful not to judge the people to whom they have

come to minister. Your kids are striving to love and serve them, so don't discourage your Goer by disrespecting their new culture. William Carey, an English missionary in the late 1700s, said that "To belong to Jesus is to embrace the nations with him."[58] Embracing the nations means seeing the people who live in those nations as image-bearers of God, because "The life of faith necessarily involves us in a worldwide community that includes strange-appearing, strange-acting and strange-sounding people."[59] Even if some of their social norms seem awkward or illogical to you, remember that you are not superior to these *strange-sounding* people, nor are they to you; you are simply different from one another. And *both* of you bear the image of God.

Missionary Mama, when you use your time, effort, finances, and energy to visit your Goer abroad, you show great support for them. You say, "Hey, I want to see what you are doing because I think it is important." Let your child lead you through their adventure and their life, because it is truly a wonderful thing to become a supporter of their dreams. And when you leave, you will be so proud you raised such an amazing human. Hug your Goer tightly and tell them so.

As you depart to head home, your heart may be heavy, so remember that beginnings and endings, meetings and departures, are always a mix of hard, happy, and bittersweet. So have those sunglasses handy and let your tears fall.

Maybe one trip is all you take to visit your Goer; you will be so glad you took it. That *one* trip will be such a gift to your child. Not only will it provide you with a clearer vision of what they are doing, but it will also bring joy to your heart—and theirs.

I hope you make the trip, sweet sister, but keep this in mind:

when you consider crossing the ocean in a cylinder made of steel, your heart may strongly say, "Nope." Just keep pushing those fears away by putting one foot in front of the other, and before long you too will be saying, "I'm doing it! I'm doing it!" while your Heavenly Father looks on and smiles.

HEART AFLOAT

No one told me when I had my perfect baby that I would have to give him up
so
many
times;
I thought he was mine to keep.
But I was wrong.
This boy I raised is not really mine;
I don't get to keep him forever.
Forever
is only
for heaven.

Things on this earth are only on loan.
I didn't know it would be like this,
how my heart would resist releasing my boy,
how much I would have to trust my Father to do his best
for my
very
precious one.

I was surprised at my utter helplessness
when I couldn't stop the clock,
when time would not stand still.
I have never truly had control.
I
just thought
I did.

It's the illusion that creates the heartache,
but memories sustain the soul
that hungers for wholeness.
And hope for a sweet reunion
keeps it
afloat
in the storm.

Because surrendering your children so many times
is like taking little pieces of your heart and
setting them
to sail
on the sea.

I wrote this poem immediately after my son went abroad as a way to process my sadness of his departure and my grief at letting him go.

CONCLUSION

No one told me when I had my perfect baby that I would have to give him up so many times; I thought he was mine to keep.

OF SWINGS AND SACRIFICES

I hadn't touched his face for twenty-two months, so when I saw him at the subway station after we disembarked, exhausted and disheveled from nearly thirty hours of traveling, I cried tears of joy. In that very instant, when I saw him emerge from the crowd to take us to the hospital where his wife and newborn daughter—our granddaughter!—were staying, my thoughts raced to a time when he was my little boy and I was pushing him on a swing while he giggled with delight. I don't know why that specific memory jumped into my brain at the moment of our reunion, but I now think it had something to do with grief.

I really loved being a mom. I really loved having my kids close around me so I could care for them, influence them, and be involved in their everyday lives. But when my firstborn went abroad to do missions in Asia, I had to give him up.

And this memory of swings, a happy one full of contentment, reminded me of what I had sacrificed when he left—the sweet melody of his giggles and the closeness of his delight. Yes, it had been years since he had actually lived at home; he had gone to college, gotten married, and even started his own business before he left the States. But he had been accessible to me. I may have had to drive hours to see him, but if I wanted to touch his now-whiskered face and kiss his head, I could do it. At our subway reunion, I vowed that, if I could help it, I would never again let nearly two years separate me from seeing my precious firstborn.

I thought he was mine to keep. But I was wrong.
This boy I raised is not really mine; I don't get to keep him
forever. Forever is only for heaven.

Though I birthed him and loved him, this man-child of mine wasn't really mine. He was God's kid doing God's work.

Things on this earth are only on loan.

We took our first visit to see him and his wife just five months after they moved abroad. My initial adjustment to his leaving the States was minimal because I knew I would see him face to face very soon. We loved experiencing the place where he and his missions-loving bride were living and working. I met their vegetable lady, ate at their favorite noodle shop, and hung out with their devoted team. This was all very good for my soul. And after we left, it was really good for my mama heart to "see him" in a specific place when we talked on the phone or he spoke of the flower shop at the end of their block.

I didn't know it would be like this, how my heart would resist releasing my boy, how much I would have to trust my Father to do his best for my very precious one.

The feeling of really missing him and his presence here in our family intensified the next summer when our youngest child graduated from high school and went away to college. Now, all four of my children were out of the home, and I was feeling lost and sad. I didn't expect the transition to him (and the rest of the kids) leaving home to be so very hard. It was a time of deep searching for me.

I was surprised at my utter helplessness when I couldn't stop the clock, when time would not stand still. I have never truly had control. I just thought I did.

Maybe my experience of being a missionary mama is different from yours. Maybe my oversized feelings are making some of you roll your eyes and call me a drama queen. But I am guessing that a few of you are feeling helpless as well and would love nothing more than to beat up Father Time.

It's really hard to release control of people we love so much.

GAINING AND LOSING

I am not saying all of my experience as the mother of a missionary has been negative. It hasn't. I have gained great joy knowing that my kids were following Jesus and that God has led them to be his ambassadors to the world! I have been motivated to be more outward with my own faith because I was impressed with the boldness of my Goer. I have probably become sturdier emotionally because I've had to deal with my fears. But it has also been a long and arduous journey of losing. It has made me more appropriately reliant on friends and family to meet new emotional needs, and it has made me yearn for community with other Missionary Mamas like you.

It's the illusion that creates the heartache, but memories sustain the soul that hungers for wholeness. And hope for a sweet reunion keeps it afloat in the storm.

When your child moves very far away from you, it shatters your illusion of wholeness. It will make your heart ache for their presence. Our kids are far away from our daily influence. This reality can be very hard to accept, and these life changes can make us feel wobbly and weird. In our peculiar suffering, we won't always understand or agree with everything our kids are doing. And others won't understand our sacrifice. But it's all a part of letting them go.

Because surrendering your children so many times is like taking little pieces of your heart and setting them to sail on the sea.

Now that your child has left, maybe you feel like you're journeying into unknown territory. Maybe this whole journey of scattering your heart is not what you wanted to do. I hear you, mama. So many times, I was you.

God has given me comfort that I want to give to you. I want to help you on the journey.

This adventure we are on is no vacation, but that doesn't mean we should avoid it. It's a thru-hike full of mud and mileage, tears and trials, but also so much joy. If you feel like you're wandering in the wilderness, you're not alone. Join the crew.

Missionary Mama, thank you for your friendship along the path. Be strong and brave and faith-full. And remember, *When you start walking, follow the footsteps of the person in front of you.*

ACKNOWLEDGMENTS

This book would not have been written without my co-author and faithful teacher, Jesus. So many days I cried out to him for clarity. Little by little he gave it to me; not all at once, because he knew that if he allowed a waterfall, I would no longer be thirsty—nor would I be dependent on him. I waited, day by day, and he showed me the next thing, and the next, and the next . . .just a trickle at a time. Sometimes waiting was hard, and I doubted that I would be able to write. I promised to provide initiative if he would supply inspiration. And since he is always faithful, even when I am not, our combined efforts became *The Missionary Mama's Survival Guide*. The journey was easier when I stopped trying to lead and, instead, agreed to follow him.

I am so grateful for the fellow hikers on this switchback trail called "publishing." First, I want to thank my husband, Brent, who encouraged me to pursue my dream when I mentioned the idea to him while we explored the Shoshone National Forest, and who often spent his evenings alone as I sequestered myself in the basement to write. Secondly, I want to thank my kids, who are good sports and even better hikers, for letting me use their stories as metaphors in my journey. I am especially indebted to my oldest son, the Goer, and his precious wife and daughter, whose journey across the ocean allowed me to learn about myself and God in a whole new way. Thirdly, though I had the idea to create something for Missionary Mamas, I couldn't have established a platform without the assistance of my local church body, Cornerstone Church of Ames, and our former missions pastor, Mike, along with my book coach, Elizabeth Trotter, whose expertise and encouragement allowed my idea to write a book for missionary moms become a reality.

I am thankful for numerous friends who read, commented, and helped me hone my manuscript, and for my handful of pre-readers who perused, evaluated, and endorsed my final copy with words of insight and praise.

I am exceptionally honored that parenting expert and author Lori Wildenberg not only agreed to write my foreword but also used a hiking analogy to make her point. I couldn't have asked for a better opener. She is a fellow hiker and like-hearted mama, and I am grateful for her.

And finally, I am thrilled to be partnering and publishing with The Upstream Collective as they expand their reach to families of missionaries. I am especially grateful for Bradley Bell, Jamie Chaplin, Hayley Moss, and David McWhite for walking me through the publication process and helping an idea in my head become this book in your hands. I am privileged to be part of their team.

About the
AUTHOR

Tori R. Haverkamp is the mother of a missionary and the editor of Parents of Goers (parentsofgoers.com), a multi-media website devoted to educating and encouraging parents of cross-cultural workers. Because of her disorienting experience of sending her son overseas, Tori desires to be an empathetic guide for those just beginning the Missionary Mama journey. With a master's degree in theological studies and over thirty years of experience in ministry, Tori speaks, writes, and teaches on motherhood, marriage, and missions. She and her husband, Brent, along with their four now-grown children, are avid backpackers. They have hiked all over the world and survived to tell great stories of their adventures.

APPENDIX

FAQS

As a new Missionary Mama, I had so many questions about the journey. You probably have some too. These are a few of the answers I have collected on the hike.

1. **How can I trust that I will be able to function normally with my child across the ocean?**

   You probably won't function normally at first. Transitions are always hard. Read this book, talk to friends, connect with other Missionary Mamas. Don't deny your grief; pray about it and let God minister to your heart. Paul David Tripp tells us to "Look for God in the hallways of your life."[60] Hallways take us out of the place we are in and into new rooms to explore.

2. **Will we ever be together as a family again? and/or How will it feel to have only part of my family here for holidays, birthdays, etc.?**

   Your Goer will be encouraged to visit his passport country at least every few years, maybe even more often. Really enjoy those times when your whole family is physically present. Breathe in the sweet scent of "normal," but don't inhale too deeply, or you will be despondent when your Goer leaves again. While your Goer is abroad, family gatherings do feel different, even if you Zoom them in, but you will adjust and learn to celebrate without them being physically present.

3. *How should I respond when other parents complain about their children moving to a new town?*

You should pause, bite your tongue, release it, and smile. Then you should probably leave and do your eye-rolling at home. Please realize, though, that loss is loss. It hurts a mama's heart to have her babies far away, even if that "far away" is only a three-hour drive.

4. *How can I continue to have a close relationship with my child when they are so far away?*

You will have to be intentional with it, but in this day and age, there are many options to help you communicate and connect with your child. Setting up a regular schedule of phone calls or video chats will help to make this happen. Since you are the parent, you may be more motivated to stay close than your child is, so take the initiative to ensure the distance doesn't threaten the strength of your relationship. Then make a plan to connect. Chapters 11 and 12 can give you some creative solutions.

5. ***Will I be able to make the trip across the ocean if I am afraid of flying? or I have never traveled internationally and don't know how to do it. Should I try it?***

Short answer: Yes, and yes. Check out Diane's story in Chapter 15. Do not let your fears rule your life. Let your faith be your leader instead.

6. ***What is my child actually doing? Are they safe?***

Your child is cooperating with God in his mission to redeem the world. It's a big job (check out Chapter 2). Who defines safe? Is anything safe? Is God even safe? In the words of Mr. Beaver from C. S. Lewis's *The Lion, the Witch, and the Wardrobe*, "'Course he isn't safe. But he's good." (For resources regarding safety, see suggestions in "The Ranger Station" appendix that follows.)

7. ***Will my grandchildren know me?***

With a bit of effort on your part, your grandchildren will both know and adore you. Maybe you won't be able to hold their chubby little hands, but you can admire their dimples and their giggles when you read them a funny story. Read Chapter 8 for some ideas of how to be present in their lives from a distance.

8. ***Who can I talk to about my grief? My friends don't understand. Is there a support group I can go to?***

Talk to a friend, talk to your spouse, talk to a pastor, talk to a counselor. Let it all out so it won't seem so threatening and you won't feel so crazy. Many of your friends won't understand, but that doesn't mean they don't love you. They would probably be more than happy to offer a listening ear. Give them a chance to do so. I haven't found a support group to help me, but I have gathered around me a group of like-hearted Missionary Mama friends by way of social media, blogging, podcasting, and some shared Zoom calls. These relationships have breathed life into my exhausting journey and given me the energy to keep hiking.

9. Will I be able to think rightly about this and not be mad at God for taking my child across the sea?

Probably not without effort and some filtered thinking (check out Chapter 4). Hard things can make us question God, but if we push through the chaos of questions, we often get to a sweet place of freedom where our hearts and minds can trust that God's plan is good.

10. Will my child miss me? Can I ask them when they will come home?

Your child will miss you, but they may not verbalize that "missing" to you. They will have to adjust to a new place and new circumstances, and doing so will make them nostalgic for what they once had. So, whether your child says "Mama, I miss you" or not, know that you are loved, valued, and missed by them. Feel free to tell them that you miss them, but don't relay it in a desperate tone. Our kids are emboldened to live their lives successfully if they believe that we, their moms, are doing well. Hold off on asking them when they will return; instead, lead the conversation with this: "Tell me about your plans for the next two/five/ten years." If they don't include a definite return date within that answer, ask if they plan to serve long-term. This conversation will open the doors to asking clearer questions so you can clarify your expectations. Tread very lightly here. A lot of parenting is done selfishly as we try to protect ourselves from pain. Let your child be separate from you, even if it's painful, and allow them to make their own choices for their life and future.

Helpful Resources
THE RANGER STATION

When you're feeling a little lost on your trip, it's always a good idea to visit the Ranger Station. Below are some tools and resources that will help you navigate your Missionary Mama journey.

COMMUNICATION TOOLS

Texting Platforms

» If you and your child both have iPhones, iMessage will probably work the best for texting. iMessage is an internet-based texting platform, so anytime you or your Goer have internet access (or Wi-Fi), an iMessage can be sent/received.

» If you have an Android device, regular texting may still work if both parties have cell service available at their locations.

» We have also found these internet-based texting/social media apps to be helpful. Some offer Wi-Fi calling as well: WhatsApp, WeChat, Google Hangouts, Signal, and Facebook Messenger.

Video Platforms

» If you and your child both have iPhones, FaceTime can be a fun way to "see" each other often. Try it the next time you call. You can use many of the internet-based texting platforms listed above for video calls as well.

» Our family has really enjoyed a video chat app called Marco Polo. It is a free way to leave a video for a family member or friend. The receiver can watch this "message" at any time (even multiple times an hour if it is from their grandchild), and they can respond at their leisure. Marco Polo also allows you to create chatting groups to share videos with the whole family or friend group.

» Snapchat is a similar media-sharing platform, except once the receiver opens the message, it disappears. The photo, video, or meme is only available for a short time before it becomes inaccessible (unlike Marco Polo videos, which are stored on the app).

» For longer calls or weekly/monthly video chats, try Skype, Zoom, or Google Meet.

Apps/Sites for Flying and Traveling Abroad

» GateGuru (gateguru.com) lets you specify an airport and then guides you to it and through it.

» FlightAware (flightaware.com) provides real-time, worldwide flight-traffic data—very helpful for knowing whether your flight is on-time.

» OFX (ofx.com) is a good option for international money transfer and currency exchange.

» Duolingo (duolingo.com) is a fun app you can install on your phone to learn a new language.

» Rosetta Stone (rosettastone.com) is a language-learning program that I found to be very helpful.

Apps/Sites to Help You Gift Your Goer

» Venmo is a good way to send fun money to your child.

» Netflix subscriptions can help them keep up with their favorite shows.

» Audible subscriptions provide a library of audio books, giving them something to listen to while walking to school or riding on the subway.

» Receiving an iTunes gift card may be music to your Goer's ears.

» An electronic Kindle book from Amazon.com may enable you to have a book club with your child or grandchild.

» Maybe your Goer prefers a quick read instead. Zinio offers over 6,000 online magazines.

» Want to go big? Try the Tinngly.com "Experience Gifts" for a never-to-be-forgotten adventure.

HELPFUL SITES AND ARTICLES

Missions

» TheUpstreamCollective.org: Upstream has a variety of free and paid resources to educate believers about missions and equip the church to better send and care for their sent ones.

» IMB.org: Check out the free courses from the International Mission Board at imb.pathwright.com/library.

» JoshuaProject.net: This site gives detailed information on people groups who still need to hear the gospel of Jesus. It is a great site to help you learn about the people in your child's host country.

» OperationWorld.org: Operation World describes itself as "The Definitive Prayer Guide to Every Nation" and offers to send you a daily email to help you pray specifically for different nations one day at a time.

» Perspectives.org: Perspectives is the fifteen-week class on World Missions I mentioned in Chapter 2. It is offered in a variety of churches and will expand your understanding of missions and the world.

Stayers and Goers

» Parents of Goers Website and Podcast

parentsofgoers.com

buzzsprout.com/1871214

This is the ministry that birthed this book. I would highly recommend joining our community!

» A Life Overseas: A Cross-Cultural Conversation

alifeoverseas.com

This site features posts from current and former missionaries and cross-cultural workers. I have found it super helpful, and it has enabled me to get a glimpse of the Goers' experience.

Other Helpful Resources

» "But Are You Safe?" Article by Rachel Pieh Jones. https://rachelpiehjones.substack.com/p/but-are-you-safe?s=r.

» "Family Support: The special role parents play in missions." Article by Scott R. Johnson. https://www.crosswalk.com//1197165.

» "The Greatest Hurdle Most Missionaries Face." Article by Darren Carlson. https://www.thegospelcoalition.org/article/the-greatest-hurdle-most-missionaries-face.

» "How to Honor Your Parents When You're Called to Missions." Article by Debbie Stephens. https://team.org/blog/how-to-honor-parents-called-missions.

» "I'm Not Called to Keep My Kids from Danger." Article by Rachel Pieh Jones. https://www.christianitytoday.com/ct/2017/november-web-only/im-not-called-to-keep-my-kids-from-danger.html.

» "Parents of Missionaries." Article by Ellen Livingood. https://catalystservices.org/parents-of-missionaries.

BOOKS TO BRIGHTEN YOUR MIND

Books for Stayers

» *Parents of Missionaries* by Cheryl Savageau and Diane Stortz

» *Parents as Partners* (a free e-book by The International Mission Board). https://www.imb.org/wp-content/uploads/2021/11/Parents-as-Partners-Supporting-Your-Family-as-They-Serve_IMB-2021.pdf

Books about Missions

» *Operation World* by Jason Mandryk

» *The 3D Gospel: Ministry in Guilt, Shame, and Fear Cultures* by Jayson Georges

» *Introducing Christian Mission Today: Scripture, History, and Issues* by Michael Goheen

Kids' Books about Missions

» *Window on the World: When We Pray God Works* by Molly Wall and Jason Mandryk

» *Parenting with a Global Vision* by Weave Families (a six-week study for parents and kids)

» Trailblazer Books by Dave and Neta Jackson (kids' books about missionaries and evangelists)

Books about Grandparenting from Afar

» *Amah Faraway* by Margaret Chiu Greanias and Tracy Subisak

»*Grandpa Across the Ocean* by Hyewon Yum

» *Long Distance Grandma* by Janet Teitsort

Books on Transitions and Emotional Health

» *Barbara and Susan's Guide to the Empty Nest* by Barbara Rainey and Susan Yates

» *Lost in the Middle: Midlife and the Grace of God* by Paul David Tripp

» *The Emotionally Healthy Woman: Eight Things You Have to Quit to Change Your Life* by Geri Scazzero

» *Made for More: An Invitation to Live in God's Image* by Hannah Anderson

Missionary Biographies

» *God's Smuggler* by Brother Andrew and John and Elizabeth Sherrill

» *Tramp for the Lord* by Corrie ten Boom and Jamie Buckingham

» *Made for the Journey: One Missionary's First Year in the Jungles of Ecuador* by Elisabeth Elliot

Helpful Scriptures to
SHOW YOU THE WAY

All the verses quoted in the book, plus an abundance of others, are here to help you think rightly about your Missionary Mama journey. (All passages are from the NIV unless otherwise noted.)

> Be strong and courageous. Do not be afraid or terrified … for the Lord your God goes with you; he will never leave you nor forsake you. (Deuteronomy 31:6)
>
> •••
>
> The beloved of the Lord rests in safety—the High God surrounds him all day long—the beloved rests between his shoulders. (Deuteronomy 33:12 NRSV)
>
> •••
>
> Sing to the Lord, all the earth; proclaim his salvation day after day. Declare his glory among the nations, his marvelous deeds among all peoples. (1 Chronicles 16:23-24)
>
> •••
>
> You make known to me the path of life: in your presence there is fullness of joy; at your right hand are pleasures forevermore. (Psalm 16:11 ESV)

Cast your burden on the Lord, and he will sustain you; he will never permit the righteous to be moved. (Psalm 55:22 ESV)

•••

I will praise God's name in song and glorify him with thanksgiving. (Psalm 69:30)

•••

Yet I am always with you; you hold me by my right hand. You guide me with your counsel, and afterward you will take me into glory. (Psalm 73:23-24)

•••

If you say, "The Lord is my refuge," and you make the Most High your dwelling, no harm will overtake you, no disaster will come near your tent. For he will command his angels concerning you to guard you in all your ways; they will lift you up in their hands, so that you will not strike your foot against a stone. (Psalm 91:9-12)

•••

When I said, "My foot is slipping," your unfailing love, Lord, supported me. When anxiety was great within me, your consolation brought me joy. (Psalm 94:18-19)

•••

For he knows how we are formed, he remembers that we are dust. (Psalm 103:14)

•••

When I called you, you answered me; you made me bold and stouthearted. (Psalm 138:3 NIV 1984)

•••

A happy heart makes the face cheerful, but heartache crushes the spirit. (Proverbs 15:13)

•••

Along unfamiliar paths I will guide them; I will turn the darkness into light before them and make the rough places smooth. These are the things I will do; I will not forsake them. (Isaiah 42:16)

...

This is what the Lord Almighty, the God of Israel, says to all those I carried into exile from Jerusalem to Babylon: "Build houses and settle down; plant gardens and eat what they produce. Marry and have sons and daughters; find wives for your sons and give your daughters in marriage, so that they too may have sons and daughters. Increase in number there; do not decrease. Also, seek the peace and prosperity of the city to which I have carried you into exile. Pray to the Lord for it, because if it prospers, you too will prosper. (Jeremiah 29:4–7)

...

But seek first his kingdom and his righteousness, and all these things will be given to you as well. (Matthew 6:33)

...

Take my yoke upon you and learn from me, for I am gentle and humble in heart, and you will find rest for your souls. For my yoke is easy and my burden is light. (Matthew 11:29–30)

...

Then Jesus came to them and said, "All authority in heaven and on earth has been given to me. Therefore go and make disciples of all nations, baptizing them in the name of the Father and of the Son and of the Holy Spirit, and teaching them to obey everything I have commanded you. And surely I am with you always, to the very end of the age." (Matthew 28:18–20)

...

"Truly I tell you," Jesus said to them, "no one who has left home or wife or brothers or sisters or parents or children for the sake of the kingdom of God will fail to receive many times

as much in this age, and in the age to come, eternal life.
(Luke 18:29–30)

...

The Word became flesh and made his dwelling among us. We have seen his glory, the glory of the one and only Son, who came from the Father, full of grace and truth. (John 1:14)

...

Not only so, but we also glory in our sufferings, because we know that suffering produces perseverance; perseverance, character; and character, hope. And hope does not put us to shame, because God's love has been poured out into our hearts through the Holy Spirit, who has been given to us.
(Romans 5:3–5)

...

How, then, can they call on the one they have not believed in? And how can they believe in the one of whom they have not heard? And how can they hear without someone preaching to them? And how can anyone preach unless they are sent? As it is written, "How beautiful are the feet of those who bring good news!" (Romans 10:14–15)

...

Do not conform to the pattern of this world, but be transformed by the renewing of your mind. Then you will be able to test and approve what God's will is—his good, pleasing and perfect will. (Romans 12:2)

...

Praise be to the God and Father of our Lord Jesus Christ, the Father of compassion and the God of all comfort, who comforts us in all our troubles, so that we can comfort those in any trouble with the comfort we ourselves receive from God. For just as we share abundantly in the sufferings of Christ, so also our comfort abounds through Christ. (2 Corinthians 1:3–5)

Therefore we do not lose heart. Though outwardly we are wasting away, yet inwardly we are being renewed day by day. For our light and momentary troubles are achieving for us an eternal glory that far outweighs them all. So we fix our eyes not on what is seen, but on what is unseen, since what is seen is temporary, but what is unseen is eternal.
(2 Corinthians 4:16–18)

...

We demolish arguments and every pretension that sets itself up against the knowledge of God, and we take captive every thought to make it obedient to Christ. (2 Corinthians 10:5)

...

Finally, brothers and sisters, whatever is true, whatever is noble, whatever is right, whatever is pure, whatever is lovely, whatever is admirable—if anything is excellent or praiseworthy—think about such things. (Philippians 4:8)

REFERENCES

Appalachian Trail Conservancy. Accessed March 28, 2022. https://appalachiantrail.org/.

Bible Gateway. *New International Version Bible*. https://www.biblegateway.com/.

Bible Hub. "4633. σκηνή (skéné): a tent." Accessed July 27, 2022. https://biblehub.com/greek/4633.htm.

BMA Missions. "Creative and Closed Access Nations: What Does It Mean?" June 24, 2019. https://bmamissions.org/creative-and-closed-access-nations-what-does-it-mean.

Center for Mission Mobilization. "Our Story." Accessed March 23, 2022. https://www.mobilization.org/about/our-story/.

Chisholm, Thomas Obediah. "Living For Jesus A Life That Is True." Hymn. 1917.

Elliot, Elisabeth. *Suffering Is Never for Nothing*. Nashville, TN: B&H Publishing Group, 2019.

Goheen, Michael. W. *Introducing Christian Mission Today: Scripture, History, and Issues*. Westmont, IL: IVP Academic, 2014.

Gresh, Dannah, host. "How to Show Strength and Dignity." Interview with Nancy DeMoss Wolgemuth. *Revive Our Hearts Podcast.* Podcast audio. June 9, 2022. https://www.reviveourhearts.com/podcast/revive-our-hearts/how-show-strength-and-dignity/.

Haverkamp, Tori. "Making the Trip." Interview with Diane Hamer. *Parents of Goers Podcast.* Podcast audio. January 31, 2022. https://www.buzzsprout.com/1871214/9985384-making-the-trip.

Hawthorne, Steven C. *Perspectives on the World Christian Movement.* Pasadena, CA: William Carey Library, 2009.

Kenan, Gil, dir. *A Boy Called Christmas.* Paramount Theaters, 2021. https://www.netflix.com/watch/81029733.

Kroeger, Kyle. "What is Customs at the Airport?" Via Travelers. Last modified April 26, 2022. https://viatravelers.com/what-is-customs-at-the-airport/.

Lewis, C. S. *A Grief Observed.* New York, NY: Harper, 1961.

Livingood, Ellen. "Parents of Missionaries." Catalyst Services. September 2019. https://catalystservices.org/parents-of-missionaries/.

Merton, Thomas. *Conjectures of a Guilty Bystander.* New York, NY: Doubleday, 1966.

Ortberg, John. *When the Game Is Over, It All Goes Back in the Box.* Grand Rapids, MI: Zondervan, 2015.

Peterson, Eugene H. *The Message: The Bible in Contemporary Language.* Colorado Springs, CO: Navpress, 2016.

---. *Run with the Horses: The Quest for Life at Its Best.* Westmont, IL: IVP Books, 2009.

Peterson, Jordan B. *12 Rules for Life: An Antidote to Chaos*. New York, NY: Penguin Books, 2019.

Plummer, Jo. "What is Business as Mission?" Business as Mission. January 14, 2015. https://businessasmission.com/what-is-bam/.

Savageau, Cheryl and Diane Stortz. *Parents of Missionaries: How to Thrive and Stay Connected When Your Children and Grandchildren Serve Cross-Culturally.* Westmont, IL: IVP Books, 2008.

Scazzero, Geri and Peter Scazzero. *The Emotionally Healthy Woman: Eight Things You Have to Quit to Change Your Life.* Grand Rapids, MI: Zondervan, 2014.

Seyan, Kieran. "Is jet lag worse traveling east rather than west?" LloydsPharmacy Online Doctor. September 10, 2018. https://onlinedoctor.lloydspharmacy.com/uk/travel-advice/jet-lag-east-or-west.

Skurka, Andrew. *The Ultimate Hiker's Gear Guide: Tools and Techniques to Hit the Trail.* Washington, D.C.: National Geographic Society, 2017.

Tripp, Paul David. *Lost in the Middle: Midlife and the Grace of God.* Wapwallopen, PA: Shepherd Press Incorporated, 2004.

The Westminster Standard. *The Kid's Catechism: An Introduction to the Shorter Catechism.* Accessed March 23, 2022. https://thewestminsterstandard.org/the-kids-catechism/.

Wright, Christopher J. H. *The Mission of God's People: A Biblical Theology of the Church's Mission.* 1st edition. Grand Rapids, MI: Zondervan Academic, 2010.

ENDNOTES

[1] Esther 4:14.

[2] "Do you sleep in a tent?" is the most common question we get when we relay our backpacking tales to non-backpackers. We sleep in tents because hotels in the wilderness are hard to find.

[3] You may disagree after you read about some of my family's annual backpacking vacations in later chapters.

[4] See Matthew 11:29.

[5] "Bear training" in the National Parks doesn't actually involve bears. It is a method of preparing hikers to protect themselves from these powerful and sometimes unpredictable forest dwellers.

[6] See Genesis 3.

[7] See Revelation 7:9.

[8] The Westminster Standard, *The Kid's Catechism: An Introduction to the Shorter Catechism*, accessed March 23, 2022, https://thewestminsterstandard.org/the-kids-catechism/.

[9] Steven C. Hawthorne, *Perspectives on the World Christian*

Movement (Pasadena, CA: William Carey Library, 2009).

[10] See Revelation 5:9.

[11] Christopher J. H. Wright, *The Mission of God's People: A Biblical Theology of the Church's Mission*, 1st ed. (Grand Rapids, MI: Zondervan Academic, 2010), 22–23.

[12] Michael. W. Goheen, *Introducing Christian Mission Today: Scripture, History, and Issues* (Westmont, IL: IVP Academic, 2014), 26.

[13] Taken from Andrew Skurka's *The Ultimate Hiker's Gear Guide: Tools and Techniques to Hit the Trail* (Washington, D.C.: National Geographic Society, 2017).

[14] I realize that mishinainae sounds nothing like missionary. This creative spelling was due to my son's childhood lisp and not his wonderful teacher, Mrs. Lowman.

[15] BMA Missions, "Creative and Closed Access Nations: What Does It Mean?" June 24, 2019, https://bmamissions.org/creative-and-closed-access-nations-what-does-it-mean.

[16] Jo Plummer, "What is Business as Mission?" Business as Mission, January 14, 2015, https://businessasmission.com/what-is-bam/.

[17] Don't let the pressure to use "safe language" keep you from communicating with your child. In the words of Hudson, a Goer in Southeast Asia, "It's always okay to say, 'I love you, and I'm thinking of you.'"

[18] Bible Hub, "4633. σκηνή (skéné): a tent," accessed July 27, 2022, https://biblehub.com/greek/4633.htm.

[19] Eugene H. Peterson, *The Message: The Bible in Contemporary Language* (Colorado Springs, CO: Navpress, 2016).

[20] There are exceptions. Missionaries sent by the International Mission Board (IMB), some NGOs, and those participating in health care missions are often fully funded by their organizations.

[21] Mike Ironside, interview by author, March 6, 2021.

[22] Center for Mission Mobilization, "Our Story," accessed March 23, 2022, https://www.mobilization.org/about/our-story/.

[23] Although missionaries usually have one primary sending church, they may also have multiple churches that partner with them through financial support, prayer, and encouragement.

[24] Wondering what a cairn is? Stay tuned; the next chapter will enlighten you.

[25] Geri Scazzero and Peter Scazzero, *The Emotionally Healthy Woman: Eight Things You Have to Quit to Change Your Life* (Grand Rapids, MI: Zondervan, 2014), 168-69.

[26] Ibid., 183-84.

[27] John Ortberg, *When the Game Is Over, It All Goes Back in the Box* (Grand Rapids, MI: Zondervan, 2015), 149.

[28] Paul David Tripp, *Lost in the Middle: Midlife and the Grace of God* (Wapwallopen, PA: Shepherd Press Incorporated, 2004.), 85.

[29] While these words are sometimes attributed to Abraham Lincoln, the original source of this quote is unknown.

[30] Cheryl Savageau and Diane Stortz, *Parents of Missionaries: How to Thrive and Stay Connected When Your Children and Grandchildren Serve Cross-Culturally* (Westmont, IL: IVP Books, 2008), 32.

³¹ *A Boy Called Christmas*, directed by Kenan Gil (Paramount Theaters, 2021), https://www.netflix.com/watch/81029733.

³² C. S. Lewis, *A Grief Observed* (New York, NY: Harper, 1961), 5.

³³ Jordan B. Peterson, *12 Rules for Life: An Antidote to Chaos* (New York, NY: Penguin Books, 2019), 233.

³⁴ Most likely Type 2 fun.

³⁵ Elisabeth Elliot, *Suffering Is Never for Nothing* (Nashville, TN: B&H Publishing Group, 2019), 93.

³⁶ Thomas Obediah Chisholm, "Living For Jesus A Life That Is True," hymn (1917).

³⁷ I think OT prophets may have been an early prototype of hippies, but without the illicit drugs and fornication.

³⁸ Eugene H. Peterson, *Run with the Horses: The Quest for Life at Its Best* (Westmont, IL: IVP Books, 2009), 151.

³⁹ Thomas Merton, *Conjectures of a Guilty Bystander* (New York, NY: Doubleday, 1966), 285.

⁴⁰ A Dagwood sandwich is a tall, multilayered sandwich made with a variety of meats, cheeses, and condiments. It is named after Dagwood Bumstead, a central character in the comic strip Blondie. I thought this comic was incredibly lame as a child, but I do remember the sandwiches.

⁴¹ Appalachian Trail Conservancy, accessed March 28, 2022, https://appalachiantrail.org/.

⁴² Long thru-hikes require resupply boxes (filled with goodies, socks, toiletries, shoes, and needed clothing). These very necessary boxes ship to points on, or close to, the trail. During my girls' trip, I shipped their resupply boxes to predetermined hostels and post offices, but sometimes general stores will receive

them as well.

[43] There are about 260 shelters scattered along the entire length of the 2,190-mile Appalachian Trail. These shelters are especially for thru-hikers and can be a blessing or a curse. They are a blessing when rain or wind threatens to make your tent uninhabitable, but they are a curse when a multitude of snoring hikers have settled in before you.

[44] Savageau and Stortz, 10.

[45] Ibid., 162.

[46] Ibid., 15.

[47] If you are too young to remember the Jetsons, you have missed some prime entertainment in the cartoon arena. I can't remember their grandma's name, but I really liked their dog, Astro.

[48] Geocaching is a fancy term for a new kind of family-friendly treasure hunt. Google it.

[49] The tree line is the edge of the habitat in which trees can grow. Beyond this line, trees can't tolerate the environmental conditions of the higher altitude.

[50] These podcasts will be like fresh air for your soul. You can listen to them at https://www.buzzsprout.com/1871214.

[51] Savageau and Stortz, 61.

[52] Dannah Gresh, host, "How to Show Strength and Dignity," interview with Nancy DeMoss Wolgemuth, Revive Our Hearts Podcast, podcast audio, June 9, 2022, https://www.reviveourhearts.com/podcast/revive-our-hearts/how-show-strength-and-dignity/.

[53] The pandemic affected everyone, regardless of their choices.

For missionaries who stayed, Covid-19 affected the way they were able to do ministry in their local context.

[54] The Apache Trail has been mostly closed since late 2019 because of landslides and other damage associated with the recent forest fires. LANDSLIDES, people!

[55] Tori Haverkamp, host, "Making the Trip," interview with Diane Hamer, Parents of Goers Podcast, podcast audio, January 31, 2022, https://www.buzzsprout.com/1871214/9985384-making-the-trip.

[56] Kyle Kroeger, "What is Customs at the Airport?" Via Travelers, last modified April 26, 2022, https://viatravelers.com/what-is-customs-at-the-airport/.

[57] Kieran Seyan, "Is jet lag worse travelling east rather than west?" LloydsPharmacy Online Doctor, September 10, 2018, https://onlinedoctor.lloydspharmacy.com/uk/travel-advice/jet-lag-east-or-west.

[58] William Carey, unknown source.

[59] Peterson, *Run with the Horses*, 179.

[60] Tripp, 74.

OTHER BOOKS FROM THE UPSTREAM COLLECTIVE:

Tradecraft: For the Church on Mission

The Sending Church Defined

Listen: How to Make the Most of Your Short-Term Mission Trip

Holding the Rope: How the Local Church Can Care for Its Sent Ones

First 30 Daze: Practical Encouragement for Living Abroad Intentionally

The MarketSpace: Essential Relationships Between the Sending Church, Marketplace Worker, and Missionary Team

Receiving Sent Ones During Reentry: The Challenges of Returning "Home" and How Churches Can Help

Multisite Missions Leadership: The Challenges and Opportunities of Leading Missions at a Multisite Church

Lent and Missions: A 40-Day Devotional

Available on Amazon and theupstreamcollective.org

Made in the USA
Columbia, SC
25 May 2023

17276174R00107